CRITICISM OF FICTION
A Study of Trends in the Atlantic Monthly *1857-1898*

CRITICISM
of
FICTION

A Study of Trends in the
ATLANTIC MONTHLY
1857-1898

by

Helen McMahon

Wingate College Library

BOOKMAN ASSOCIATES : NEW YORK

Copyright, 1952, Bookman Associates, Inc.

PRINTED IN THE UNITED STATES OF AMERICA
BY RECORD PRESS, NEW YORK

FOREWORD

AMONG THE MANY METHODS OF APPROACHING THE COMPLEX history of fiction, a valid one, it would seem, is the analysis of the fictional standards of a major periodical. The *Atlantic Monthly* is such a periodical. For, as Frank Luther Mott has suggested, "... the student of American magazines since 1857, whatever his predilections, is forced to agree that throughout much of its career it has maintained a higher literary standard than its contemporaries." Since a number of its critics during the second half of the nineteenth century were novelists themselves and were thus doubly interested in fictional theory and practice, its criticism of fiction deserves special attention.

Likewise, the period from 1857 until the close of the century is a profitable one for discussion, for during these years the novel was becoming increasingly aware of itself. In fact, the year 1857 marks not only the founding of the *Atlantic*; it might be said to mark as well the beginning of modern fiction, for it was in 1857 that *Madame Bovary* was published. *Atlantic* critics were well aware of the new fictional developments of the period. And they were aware, too, of the need for a criticism which, in the words of George Parsons Lathrop, would keep "pace with the novel in its more recent manifestations," which would be something more than an expression of the "chance critic's chance taste." Thus Lathrop asks for a criticism that will "penetrate the significance of the novel" and "determine some of the principles by which its further progress should be guided."

Criticism of Fiction

Since the aim of this study is an analysis of fictional theory, the materials have been organized around the chief issues involved in the criticism of fiction during the period. But within such a framework an attempt has been made to include other matters which may contribute something to our knowledge of the history of fiction. Thus as much chronological data as possible has been supplied by careful documentation and by the inclusion of a register of reviews and critical essays. Since we are dealing here with practical criticism, it has seemed useful, also, to identify the authors whose works serve as illustrations of critical precepts. For to make such identifications is to offer at least an indirect picture of literary taste as indicated by reputations. Finally, as much attention as is possible within the general framework has been given to the critics themselves. For Howells, James, and Perry, whose criticism has already been studied, such a method may serve to focus attention upon the *Atlantic* phase of their work. For Lathrop and Scudder, whose writing has not yet received study, it may allow for a partial introduction to their critical positions.

Relation of these issues to the larger pattern of intellectual and critical history is a problem which is only suggested here, for it is one which deserves separate study. But it is hoped that through the ordering of a rather large body of materials and the formulation of some statement of fictional theory during this forty year period we shall be in a better position to approach such complex problems as the relation of science, for instance, to fictional theory.

A word should perhaps be said about the organization of the issues themselves. That many of them are related to the rise of realism will be at once apparent. In fact, realism must be seen, not as one issue among several, but as an underlying issue related to such seemingly different problems as the

Foreword

structure of the novel and the novel's relation to society. Many of these aspects overlap. But some division is necessary for discussion, and this division can best be made on the basis of the underlying principles to which the various issues point. Emphasis on accurate portrayal of scene leads to a consideration of what is meant by realism, surface actuality or a more Platonic reality. The desire for life-like characters, on the other hand, bears a closer relationship to form and structure, for the emphasis on real persons leads to a demand for a strict cause and effect pattern of action. This cause and effect logic is, in turn, linked to a sense of drama and to a subsequent insistence on dramatic presentation. Many of the remarks on the illusion of reality to be gained by the banishment of the intrusive author are likewise related to form; others, which deal with didacticism, may be better studied under the general heading of the relation of the novel to society.

This study was originally submitted as a doctoral dissertation at the University of Iowa, and I wish once more to thank those who had a part in its direction. I am also grateful to the *Atlantic* for allowing me to make liberal use of quotations.

CONTENTS

Foreword — 5

Chapter One: Patterns of Realism in the *Atlantic* — 11

Chapter Two: The Structure of the Realistic Novel — 39

Chapter Three: The Realistic Novel and Society — 63

Chapter Four: Some Conclusions — 85

Notes — 103

Register of Reviews and Critical Essays — 137

Index — 181

CHAPTER ONE

PATTERNS OF REALISM IN THE ATLANTIC

CRITICAL INTEREST IN REALISM IN FICTION BEGINS EARLY IN THE *Atlantic,* appearing for the first time, in fact, in the second issue of the magazine as a reviewer writes in December, 1857: "It is refreshing to see that the German literary taste is becoming gradually more *realistic,* pure and natural, turning its back on the romantic school of the French."[1] Six months later, in May, 1858, a critic writing of George Eliot's *Scenes of Clerical Life,* speaks of the author's "just appreciation of the romance of reality" and pays tribute to the way in which "the fictitious element is securely based upon a broad groundwork of actual truth, truth as well in detail as in general."[2] "To copy Nature faithfully and heartily is certainly not less needful when stories are presented in words than when they are told on canvas or in marble,"[3] writes the reviewer.

Many of the other early reviews likewise commend "naturalness"[4] of scenes and characters and call attention to "accurate observation."[5] E. P. Whipple, for instance, in an article on Hawthorne in May, 1860, states that "the most obvious excellence" of *The Marble Faun* is "the vivid truthfulness of its descriptions of Italian life, manners, and scenery."[6] C. E. Norton, reviewing *Mademoiselle Mori; a Tale of Modern Rome* in June of the same year, comments that "the descriptions which the book contains of Roman scenes and places are full of truth, and render the common, every-day aspects of streets and squares,

11

of gardens and churches, of popular customs and social habits, with equal spirit and fidelity. The interest of the story is sustained by the distinctness with which the localities in which it passes are depicted." [7]

"Marvelous fidelity of dialect, costume, and landscape" [8] is a term of praise used by James Russell Lowell in September, 1860. The following year E. P. Whipple commends "the faithful representation of real facts and localities" [9] in the novel *Cecil Dreeme* by Theodore Winthrop. And in January, 1862, G. S. Hillard comments that Cooper's *The Spy* had "the charm of reality; it tasted of the soil." [10]

It is in Whipple's review in 1862 of *The Pearl of Orr's Island,* by Harriet Beecher Stowe, that some of the most appreciative comments on realistic tendencies occur. Noting that "Mrs. Stowe is never more in her element than in depicting unsophisticated New England life," Whipple praises the book for the "freshness, clearness, and truth of its representation, both of Nature and of persons." Not only do the author's "accurate observation" and "delicate spiritual perception" receive attention but also her ability "to impress us with a sense of the substantial reality of what she makes us mentally see." He commends likewise her "foundation of the story in palpable realities which every Yankee recognizes as true the moment they are presented to his eye." [11]

As the name for a specific literary movement, the term "realism" is used for the first time in April, 1862, in an article entitled "Foreign Literature," in which the writer speaks of realism as the attempt made by Balzac, Flaubert, and Champfleury to "incarnate in letters Nature as it is, without adornings, without ideal additions." Thus he opposes it to the "excess of fancy," to "the paradox and overdrawn scenes" of such writers as Houssaye and Capefigue. And though he is suspicious of several characteristics of this "so-called school of nature"—its "audacities," its "false air of truth," and its "extravagances"— he turns to it from the artificialities of romanticism with some relief. "As we wander among those opera swains in silk hose and those shepherdesses in satin bodices, their perfumes tire and nauseate, till we fairly wish for a good breeze wafted from some farm yard . . . ,"[12] he writes.

Recognition of French realism cannot be said to take place in the *Atlantic* for another decade, however, for it is not until 1871 that Thomas Sergeant Perry's notices become a regular feature. But during the 1860's attention continues to be paid to accurate portrayal of "incidents and characters . . . drawn from the daily life that is going on around us."[13] Thus Charles Nordhoff, writing of Theodore Winthrop in August, 1863, finds that author "an appreciative observer of everyday life. . . . He valued and understood the peculiar life and peculiar Nature of this continent," writes Nordhoff, "and like a true artist and poet, chose to represent that life and Nature of which he was a part."[14] And Thomas Wentworth Higginson, suggesting that Harriet E. Prescott's "lavish wealth of description would be a gaudy profanation, were it not based on a fidelity of observation which is Thoreau-like, so far as it goes," states that "the basis of all good writing is truth in details."[15]

By the time that William Dean Howells begins to write for the *Atlantic* in 1866 there is, then, a tendency to give frequent mention to faithful representation of actual life and to find new interest in the "acts, struggles, and suffering of the world that lies at our feet, discarding the idealizing charm which arises from distance in space or remoteness in time."[16] Howells' first *Atlantic* review of a work of fiction, Bayard Taylor's *The Story of Kennett*, gives further approval to this tendency, for Howells finds the author's "strict fidelity to place and character" far more acceptable "than the aerial romance which cannot light in any place known to the gazeteer." "Indeed," he writes, "nothing can be better than the faithful spirit in which Mr. Taylor seems to have adhered to all the facts of the life he portrays." "There is such shyness," he continues, "among American novelists (if we may so classify the writers of our meager fiction) in regard to dates, names, and localities, that we are glad to have a book in which there is great courage in this respect." [17]

The fidelity to place which Howells notes is, of course, one of the characteristics of "local color" writing, a stage in the development of realism which received considerable attention in the *Atlantic*. The term itself is used first in 1864 in a comment on George Eliot's *Romola,* as a reviewer writes: "The *couleur locale* is marvelous; nothing could be more delightfully real, for example, than the scene which transpires in Nello's barber's-shop." [18] And three years later it is again used in an essay on the Italian novels of T. Adolphus Trollope. The critic, H. T. Tuckerman, piles up phrases of commendation for Trollope, whom he calls a "Flemish artist": "most accurate and detailed reflections of local characteristics," "vigilant observation and patient record," "graphic fidelity which takes us into the heart of the people," "wholesome interest in the real life around him," and "faithful local coloring." [19] Bret Harte is the first American to whom the term is applied, as he is said, in January, 1868, to depict San Francisco with "all the advantages of local color." [20] In November of the same year Howells uses the phrase in writing of Edward Everett Hale's *If, Yes, and Perhaps,* a book in which he finds "the plot as bizarre and grotesque as you like but the people . . . all true to nature." He characterizes Mr. Hale, "after Dr. Holmes," as "the writer most deeply imbued with local colors and flavors." [21]

In some of these reviews it appears that intellectual curiosity, rather than literary standards, serves as the basis for favorable criticism. As the abundant mention of travel books in the *Atlantic* indicates, excitement about new places was in the air during these years, and certain of the literary reviews themselves indicate the current desire for geographical information. Thus Howells, in his notice of William Baker's *The New Timothy*, is forced to admit that as a story the work "is not much, but as a study of life little known to literature, it is most successful and commendable." [22] A similar note of interest in the material itself is found in the review of William Flagg's *A Good Investment; a Story of the Upper Ohio*, where it is acknowledged that even if the book "were not the interesting fiction that it is, it would be worth reading for its local truth." [23]

But perhaps the chief element responsible for the interest in local color was the combination of romance and realism which it offered. Critics might plead for real localities and for real people, but they were not averse to a "glamour of romance . . . with which the realism does not discord." [24] In dealing with regions far enough removed from every-day experience to offer a certain romantic charm and with the recent past rather than with the immediate present, local color offered a gradual transition to realism which undoubtedly made that movement more palatable to many readers. Such a combination of romantic and realistic standards is evident in a review in 1872 of *Oldtown Fireside Stories, Kate Beaumont,* and *The Hoosier Schoolmaster,* which begins: "In three works of fiction lately published we have some very faithful studies of American life in the principal phases which it once showed, and which the events of not many years have put quite out of sight if not out of being." Praising Mrs. Stowe's treatment of "a whole Yankee village world, the least important figure of which savors of the soil and 'breathes full East,'" the critic adds, "The virtues of fifty or more years ago, the little local narrowness and intolerance, the lurking pathos, the hidden tenderness of a rapidly obsolescent life, are all here, with the charm of romance in their transitory aspects." [25]

However, another review in the same year suggests that the use of such subject matter may be only a necessary step toward treating the present in literature. "Gradually, but pretty surely, the whole varied field of American life is coming into view in American fiction; not the life of this moment, but that of a half score of years ago, or a generation or two generations since," writes the critic. "And though we should like best to have the very present reproduced, we are grateful for what is done, and recognize the value of each sincere performance." [26]

It is through sincerity of performance, through treatment of "credible and recognizable people" who "pre-eminently help to verify" [27] any given locality that critics begin to realize that "the variations of life in America afford immense opportunity to the novelist." [28] The only detailed treatment of nationalism is found in an article in 1870 by Thomas Wentworth Higginson entitled "Americanism in Literature," in which the author notes that it is only since Emerson led the way with his "humblebee" that we "have dared to be American" and "to make our allusions to natural objects, real not conventional" ones. But though he finds that it is the "daring Americanism of subject" of Cooper and Mrs. Stowe that has given these writers popularity abroad, his standard is one that combines locality and universality. "The truly cosmopolitan writer," he suggests, "is not he who carefully denudes his work of everything occasional and temporary, but he who makes this local coloring forever classic through the fascination of the dream it tells." [29]

A similar absence of chauvinism is the mark of other comments on the subject, though critics are glad to call attention to the fictional possibilities offered by American subjects. Howells bases one source of his pleasure in Judd's *Margaret* on the fact that it is "singularly American," [30] and he notes, too, that Constance Fenimore Woolson's story "St. Clair Flats" offers a "not at all discouraging example of what our strangely varied American real life can do in the way of romance." [31] Horace Scudder, reviewing G. W. Cable's *The Grandissimes,* remarks that the book "shows how fine a field there is for the American novelist who will give us a local story with national relations." [32] And T. S. Perry finds in Woolson's *Rodman the Keeper* "an interesting proof of the abundance of unused material in our unwieldy country, that is simply awaiting the novelist to put it into shape and give it standing." [33] But though Perry notes that "the local color is very well given" in *John Andross* by Rebecca Harding Davis, he adds that here is "an American novel in which the American part does not outweigh everything else." [34] And a few years later he suggests that "literature has been possibly not so much enriched as enlarged by the very faithful studies of a form of society that is steadily retreating before advancing civilization." [35]

If any proof is needed that national pride has little to do with the reception accorded to realistic and local color works during these years, it can be found in the almost equal pleasure taken, during the same period, in the works of such foreign writers as Björnson and Auerbach. For just as one reaction against romanticism had manifested itself in a desire for the real and the local instead of the remote and the exotic, so another can be seen in the attention to "simplicity" and in the "blissful sense of escape from the jejune inventions and stock repetitions of what really seems a failing art with us," [36] as

Howells puts it in 1870. After much American fiction which seems to have "no middle ground between magnificent drawing rooms and the most unpleasant back alleys" the study of "humble but decent folk" [37] comes as a relief. And it is a relief, too, for the "veteran novel reader, in whom the chords of feeling have been rasped and twanged like fiddle-strings by the hysterical performances of some of our authoresses" [38] to find stories told quietly and simply. "What we lack," writes Harriet Waters Preston, complaining some years later of "the writers who make our hearts bleed, and those others who make our nerves quiver," is "calm and freshness." [39]

This calm and freshness, coupled with a sense of reality, is responsible for much of the appeal of certain foreign writers during the 1870's. Howells, reviewing Björnson's *Arne, The Happy Boy,* and *The Fisher Maiden,* commends the simple telling of simple stories. From Björnson, he writes, "we learn . . . that the finest poetry is not ashamed of the plainest fact, that the lives of men and women, if they be honestly studied, can, without surprising incident or advantageous circumstance, be made as interesting in literature as are the smallest private affairs of the men and women in one's own neighborhood; that telling a thing is enough and explaining it too much; and that the first condition of pleasing is a generous faith in the reader's capacity to be pleased by natural and simple beauty." [40] Similar qualities are found in Ruffini's *Carlino,* which the reviewer calls "of a kind of fiction—simple, direct, and confident, like that of Auerbach, Björnson, and Erckmann-Chatrian,—which no one born to speak English has yet had the courage to attempt. . . ." [41] It is a group to which Hjalmar H. Boyesen, who writes "an idyllic story which regards simple things naturally but at the same time poetically," [42] also belongs. To Thomas Sergeant Perry there is more "poetical truth and beauty" [43] in those stories of George Sand which deal with the country where the author spent her childhood than in much of her other work. Howells praises Hans Christian Andersen on the grounds of "simplicity and reality." [44] To Horace Scudder there is to be found in the "new realistic wonder-story" of Andersen, as in "the new novel," "a deeper sense of life and a finer perception of the intrinsic value of common forms." [45]

Simplicity and the value of common forms; the appeal of being "unmistakably true to life"; [46] and the charm of "a complete novelty and a distinctive coloring and atmosphere of their own" [47]—these values seen in certain foreign works continue to occupy critical attention as the work of Sarah Orne Jewett, Mary Noailles Murfree, Mary E. Wilkins, and George Washington Cable achieves popularity. That her stories are "told with a sincerity, a simplicity of manner, and a closeness of observation that recalls the rare gift of Thomas Hardy" [48] is a typical tribute to Miss Murfree. Lathrop is likewise expressing a view frequently repeated when he writes in 1884 of Miss Jewett's stories, "One can scarcely imagine anything that should approach more closely to real occurrences than these do." [49] And there is much the same praise for other local color writers.

But despite the consistent emphasis on simplicity and objective reality, critics recognize certain weaknesses that often accompany that emphasis. Thus Howells writes in 1872 of *The Hoosier Schoolmaster* that the story is "chiefly noticeable . . . as a picture of manners hitherto strange to literature, and the characters are interesting as part of the picture of manners rather than as persons whose fate greatly concerns us." [50] *Brave Hearts,* a novel dealing with California mining life, seems to be written "too much for the purpose of exhibiting special manners of mining-life, without enough of character development to make them worth representation." [51] The exploitation of

19

strangeness in manners and customs is also an issue in the review of Eggleston's *The Circuit Rider,* where such exploitation is related to the larger problem of the exclusion of the author from his work. Although Eggleston is said to have "truthfully painted the conditions and people whom he aimed to portray," he is guilty, in the eyes of the critic, of placing "an inartistic stress upon unimportant details of dialect, customs, and characters." "The novelist's business," states Howells, "is to paint such facts of character and custom as he finds so strongly that their relative value in his picture will be apparent at once to the reader without a word of comment; otherwise his historical picture falls to the level of the panorama, with a showman lecturing upon the striking points and picking them out for observance with a long stick." [52]

But writers had long been used to a more elastic tradition in fiction than that which Howells suggests. They had had, for instance, fairly free reign in the matter of landscape description, with a "pre-Raphaelite style of scenery painting in words" often a characteristic of novels, "especially such as are written by women." [53] It was a problem which local color was to intensify, for the personal appeal of a well-loved section of the country or the curiosity for pictures of life and surroundings new to literature made of description an added temptation.

Atlantic critics do not give up their delight in faithful delineation of scene. Howells, for instance, writes in 1877 of *Deephaven* that "the bits of New England landscape . . . scattered throughout these studies vividly localize them." [54] "But a fine feeling for landscape and touch in depicting it can, after all, only serve a novelist for the adorning of a tale," states Harriet Waters Preston in 1878. And she reminds her readers that "ornament, as we are incessantly informed nowadays, ought always to be restrained and subordinate to the purpose of the work." [55] Horace Scudder gives similar warning. "In fiction, where the mind is eager to get at people, it is impatient of anything but the broadest landscape effect; in poetry . . . where it lies open to suggestions, to subtle parallelisms of life and nature, it delights in detail. . . ." [56]

It is Mary Noailles Murfree who is most frequently accused of working "her moon too hard," [57] of being "wasteful of words just where words should be employed with the greatest care, in the representation of natural scenes." [58] However, Scudder and Lathrop are both willing to recognize the close connection that the author's characters bear to their environment. Lathrop's review of *In the Tennessee Mountains* notes that each story seems to have an idea "arising spontaneously out of the conditions of the peculiar community depicted." [59] Scudder states that the landscape passages in *The Prophet of the Great Smoky Mountains* are "not obstructive" but help to suggest "the spiritual meaning of the movements going on in this little world." [60] Nevertheless, he is glad to note in 1892 that Miss Murfree "is gradually condensing her expression of inanimate nature and heightening her human effects." [61]

The increased use of dialect, as authors sought to portray faithfully the persons of their stories, was also of concern to *Atlantic* critics. The popularity of dialect by 1878 is indicated by T. S. Perry's review of *The Two Circuits; a Story of Illinois Life,* a book by J. L. Crane. Perry writes, "For a few years almost nothing more has been needed for the success of an American novel than a lively record of adventure in the wilder parts of the country, with a good deal of such local color as is given by bad grammar and worse spelling that shall represent the dialectic peculiarities of the region in which the scene of the story is laid." [62] *Atlantic* critics are happy for faithfulness of dialect; Howells, for instance, reports that the speech of

Miss Jewett's characters is "rendered with a delicious fidelity." [63] But artistic discretion is also a standard. Thus Lathrop writes, also of Miss Jewett, that her people "talk idiomatically with just a hint of dialect, which is hardly dialect and does not become a stumbling block." [64] Scudder remarks that "both Miss Wilkins and Miss Jewett recognize the very subordinate value of dialect. They give just enough to flavor the conversation." [65] Scudder's comment on Kate Chopin's *Bayou Folk* makes explicit his distinction between art and scientific accuracy as he praises Miss Chopin for being "discreet enough to give suggestions of the soft, harmonious tongue to which Bayou folk have reduced English speech and not to make contributions to philology." [66] Charles Miner Thompson, writing in 1895 gives even more specific advice: "Surely the proper course, in works not avowedly scientific, is to use only as much of local peculiarity of speech as will give proper dramatic value to the talk of a character, as will not confuse the eye with queer spelling, or render any remark unintelligible without special knowledge." [67]

Exploitation of scene, custom, and dialect appear, then, as special problems within the pattern of realism, new dangers to be guarded against. Perhaps a more important danger, however, is the dullness and banality which may come from treating in fiction the average and prosaic. Though much of the realism noted thus far has been touched with at least a mild sugarcoating of romance, Howells' plea for a treatment of the "average" is not absent from *Atlantic* critical notices. "We should like, now, to have a little of the amusing insipidity, the admirable dullness, of real life depicted in fiction," [68] writes a critic in 1870. W. H. Bishop, in an article in 1879, suggests that "the most enlightened field of the novel is in social history, —to portray James K. Jackson and Elizabeth May Johnson in relation to their surroundings and times, as the formal historians do Napoleon Bonaparte and Katherine of Aragon." [69] And George Parsons Lathrop, noting that "our heroes and heroines are taken from the rank and file of the race, and represent people whom we daily encounter," states that "there is no escaping the thoughtful and elevating influence of this." "Nor need there be any implication of littleness or dullness in these aims," he adds, suggesting that "this choice of the frequent is most favorable to a true discrimination of qualities in character." [70]

But although there is frequent praise for books which "bear a likeness to the ordinary occurrences of daily life," [71] which offer truthful pictures of "commonplace village life," [72] there is also a suggestion that emphasis on commonplace, prosaic conditions may frequently result in commonplaceness of treatment. Henry James writes in 1870, "We are forever complaining, most of us, of the dreary realism, the hard, sordid, pretentious accuracy, of the typical novel of the period, of the manner of Trollope, or that of Wilkie Collins, of that, in our own country, of such writers as the author of *Hedged In* and the author of *Margaret Howth*." James pleads, instead, "for a little romance, a particle of poetry, a ray of the ideal." [73] "Naturalness is not enough," complains a reviewer in 1873 in discussing the work of Jean Ingelow, when it is "displayed in the wearying gossip and *badinage* of an extremely ordinary set of people." [74]

"Perhaps the most inane thing ever put forth in the name of literature," writes Charles Dudley Warner in an essay "Modern Fiction" in 1883, "is the so-called domestic novel." Characterizing such writings as "the doughnut of fiction," he insists that "it needs genius to import into literature ordinary conversation, petty domestic details, and the commonplace and vulgar phases of life." [75] Warner's views are shared by both

Perry and Scudder. Perry is willing to grant that since the days of Sir Walter Scott we have learned "precision, completeness of detail, and the analysis of passion," but he often becomes impatient with the "literary pre-Raphaelitism" of authors who "take a brief period and generally commonplace people and describe a few tepid passions that flourish in every block in the street."[76] Scudder's review of Stockton's stories reveals a similar distaste for this phase of current realistic fiction, for his pleasure in Stockton comes from the "mockery" of realism which he finds in that author. Stockton is unlike those realists who allow their characters "to break all the ten commandments in turn but use their most strenuous endeavor to keep them from breaking the one imperious commandment, Thou shalt not transgress the law of average experience."[77]

Of Howells' own treatment of ordinary experience Scudder suggests that the chief fault perhaps lies in the narrowness of range. Reviewing *Indian Summer* in 1886 he writes, "Sparrows, orioles, wrens, are all engaging little creatures and one may observe them with great delight; but after all, an ornithologist may make a mistake who looks with all his might and main at some chattering English sparrows, when likely as not there is a flight overhead of some strong-winged wild geese sweeping northward after a southern hibernation or possibly even some hawks poising in upper air for a downward swoop."[78]

It is literalness of treatment, however, which is the basis for much of the criticism of realism. And it is Anthony Trollope who is one of the chief offenders, for though his "sober fidelity to nature" and his "sound sense of reality" are granted, it is suggested that his sense of reality may come in part from the very "narrowness of [his] imagination."[79] It is admitted that Trollope has "learned much in what is called the realist school," but there seems to be much about fiction that he does not know.

He "has not taken lessons in psychology"; his "insight is anything but profound"; and he shows but "little preoccupation with spiritual questions." "Literalness of perception" and "simple observation" are other accusations made against him, and it is declared that he is "conscious of seeing the surface of things so clearly, perhaps, that he deems himself exempt from all profounder obligations." [80]

Reviewing *Phineas Redux* in May, 1874, Perry admits the "resemblance to life," the way in which "the people come and go and think and talk very much as do our neighbors and friends." But he complains that Trollope "never sees beneath the words and gestures of his characters," that "he has a keen eye for little social by-play but there he stops." Such surface realism kills the imagination, Perry believes, giving us only the "recognition of familiar objects." "We look at a mirror instead of a picture," he adds, dismissing Trollope's books as useful to our grandchildren for their "photographic accuracy." [81] That the books are "photographically true" but not "imaginatively true" [82] is likewise Scudder's verdict. To Lathrop, Trollope gives evidence of "how thoroughly demoralizing" literalism of this kind may become. Guilty of accumulating "irrelevances with a persistence proving him to be for verisimilitude before all things," Trollope, in Lathrop's opinion, "will construct a long story out of atomic particles, making it as densely compact as a honey-comb with the honey left out." [83] And E. P. Whipple gives facetious sanction to the charge of "daguerreotypy" as he writes that Trollope "will never fail for subjects as long as the kingdom of Great Britain and Ireland contains thirty millions of people, 'mostly bores,' and as long as he has his mental daguerreotype machine in order." [84]

The dislike for photographic realism, or literalism, which is expressed in the criticism of Trollope is, of course, an expression of the anti-aesthetic dangers which these critics see in the new movement. For they fear that the novel, in becoming a literal recording of facts, may cease to become an art form and degenerate into mere report or journalism. Perry and Scudder also fear the encroachment of science on fiction. "We have caught the scientific spirit in literature," writes Scudder in 1891, adding that "the prevailing temper of the realistic school . . . is in literature what specialization is in science." [85] But the danger had been recognized ten years before when Perry had faced Zola's denial of the imagination. The encouragement which Zola gives to novelists for the "careful study of life" [86] is never questioned by Perry, who is responsible for much of the criticism of French fiction. When Zola "shows the flimsy unreality of Hugo's *Ruy Blas* he does good work." [87] And Perry is even willing to concede that the "ultimate effect" of *Nana* on fiction "may be a good one, by making people study life instead of fantastic problems and fantastic people." [88] But the scientific attitude of the group represented by Zola is a different matter. For though Perry grants that "the new men, who are scientific, have, to be sure, the merit of doing something and that rightly counts for something," he also believes that "it may be that readers will look for something besides scientific method in the fiction that is provided for them." [89] Zola's attempt "to beat the scientific man with his own weapons," his belief that art is "as obsolete as the notion that the world is flat" [90] meet, in fact, with Perry's blunt disapproval. "Now to assert that the imagination is an obsolete thing is like saying that henceforth perspective must never be used in pictures, because it is of the nature of deception; that artists must content themselves with arranging things in different actual planes," writes Perry. To the American critic, Zola "strays from his bent when he blames all use of the imagination and observes that the novel writer can busy himself solely with observed facts." For though Perry is willing to concede that "imagination, without a substratum of truth to nature, is apt to become simply melodramatic," he believes as firmly that "with truth to nature it gives us the masterpieces of all the literature of various times." [91]

Observation, on the other hand, with its accompanying quantitative or accumulative method, seemed not likely to produce the masterpieces desired. "Balzac," writes Henry James in 1871, "dreamed of transmitting to future ages a perfect image of the France of his day and created for the purpose that ponderous mechanism among whose derricks and scaffolds we wander now as among the pillars and arches of a dim cathedral." [92] And in 1874 Lathrop also suggests that Balzac "is often too matter-of-fact, or too statistical, in his statement of characters, situations, and appearances." [93] According to Perry, Flaubert, in *La Tentation de Saint Antoine,* illustrates the same dependence on facts. There is, to be sure, "an appearance of accuracy, but it is an accuracy that exists for itself, to endure criticism, much more than to call up any feeling in the reader, except one of amazement at the author's industry." "A more fervent imagination," writes Perry, "would have aided the dramatic part of the book, and would have rendered unnecessary the enormous accumulation of details." [94] Of Flaubert's *Trois Contes* Perry notes in 1877 that "insignificant details are crowded into every page but simply for their own sake." [95]

Nor is greater success achieved by Zola who "simply takes down the side of the house—a disorderly house—and lets the reader see and hear what was going on under its roof." [96] The "collection of facts may be complete and exact but the way he has put them together is clumsy in the extreme," [97] writes Perry. And though Zola's books "will be invaluable for the statistician in future ages," they "contain not one memorable representation of some grand passion." To Perry "all the description of all the back streets and roofs in Paris will never make up for the absence of this." "But, of course, it may come in time," [98] he adds.

The failure of observation and documentation to achieve desired ends is also noted in the historical novel which, in relying heavily on research, was open to some of the same errors which characterized the work of the French realists. Although in one sense the historical novel represents a reaction against realism, especially that dealing with everyday commonplaces, it is, on the other hand, a form peculiarly susceptible to realism, one which frequently has "recourse to laborious and wearisome details wherewith to establish verisimilitude." [99] Historical accuracy was, of course, considered important, but in such a writer as William Waldorf Astor it seemed to Scudder as if "the author's historical knowledge were always getting the better of his art as a novelist." [100] And Henry James, speaking of George Eliot's *Romola,* suggests that "a twentieth of the erudition would have sufficed if there had been more of the breath of the Florentine streets. . . ." [101]

It is not entirely unexpected, therefore, that novelists like Howard Pyle and Mary Hartwell Catherwood, who draw their pictures with broader brushes, should appeal to critics wearied by research and details. "Without troubling himself about petty details, Mr. Pyle has contrived to keep the reader easily aware of the actual time of the story and to invest the tale with a true atmosphere," [102] writes Scudder in 1886. And though it seems clear to him that Miss Catherwood "has studied minutely the substratum of historical and scenic fact," he finds that "her success is due to her power of conceiving human life, her fidelity to the truth of that inner fact which is independent of time, place, and circumstance, yet which becomes real to us when it is clothed by the imagination in its fitting exterior form." [103] History passed "through the alembic of fine poetic imagination" [104] rather than that which attempts "to give a quality of truthfulness by the use of irrelevant minutiae" [105] is Scudder's standard. Thus he is in at least partial agreement with Harriet Waters Preston, who believes that "the old-fashioned historical novel, preposterous as it seems when judged by the standards of modern criticism," at least left "a distinct impression on the mind," an effect that perhaps "the labored realism" and "the anatomical studies of the present" do not always have.[106]

In making these reservations against realism, *Atlantic* critics are not, by any means, denying the importance of actual detail which they had stressed earlier. The "rich density of detail" [107] which Henry James had found attractive in the works of George Eliot in 1866 remains a standard. James speaks of Daudet as "a passionate observer . . . not perhaps of the deepest things in life but of the whole realm of the immediate, the expressive, the actual," and adds that "the new fashion of realism has indeed taught us all that in any description of life the description of places and things is half the battle." [108] Perry, admiring at least some of the work of Gustave Droz, notes in 1875 how that author "takes pains to mention insignificant trifles which, while they appear trivial, are surest to carry conviction," how he "always writes with that most truthful realism which is the height, or at least one of the heights, of art. . . ." [109] To Lathrop, likewise, the need for realism is not to be questioned, for it not only "supplies the visual distinctness which is one of the great charms of the stage" but is also necessary as a part of the study of human nature. "With his investigation of psychological phenomena or insight into the mysteries of spiritual being," Lathrop writes, the author "must unite the study of all that accompany these in the individual: as corporeality, with that curious net-work of appearances, habits, opinions in which each human person is enveloped." [110]

But whatever the importance of realistic details, the actual truth observed by the artist is only part of the author's equipment. He must be able to do more than merely observe accurately. Thus James speaks of Gustave Droz as "a master of what we may call sensuous detail; he thoroughly understands the relation between the cultivated fancy and the visible, palpable facts of the world." [111] And he notes in Daudet not only skill in observation but also "a delicate, constant sense of beauty," a sense that distinguishes him from Zola. [112] But it is George Parsons Lathrop who gives the most decisive statement that art is something more than literal or scientific recording. To Lathrop, "mere transcription of facts, aspects, and phases observed by the writer is—we find it necessary, notwithstanding its self-evidence, once more to announce—neither artistry nor anything approaching it." Such transcription he would not even call "realism." To him it is, instead, mere "literalism." For he believes that "realism sets itself at work to consider characters and events which are apparently the most ordinary and uninteresting, in order to extract from these their full value and true meaning." He continues, "In short, realism reveals. Where we thought nothing worthy of notice, it shows everything to be rife with significance." [113]

To extract this "full value and true meaning" is the task of the imagination. As used by Lathrop and Perry, the term "imagination" refers to something other than the mere inventive faculty which produces the works of romanticism. It is to them a kind of insight, an "anterior vision" which appeals to "the mind behind the eye," [114] which reveals the meaning of the fact. To Lathrop the highest function of the imagination is "the conception of things in their true relation." [115] Sometimes the emphasis is chiefly aesthetic, with the term "imagination" used to indicate the author's ability to dramatize a situation in order to reveal its significance or to give to his facts, by means of careful selection, a kind of symbolic force. Sometimes it seems to be a matter of the author's insight into life, his awareness of the relation of the particular to the universal. To Lathrop, writers like "Thackeray, George Eliot, Hawthorne, Balzac, Turgénieff possess distinct points of view from which to contemplate the revolving world. Pausing at some standpoint of ideal perception, they let the variety of life pass under their eyes, and translate its meanings into the new language of their new genius." Others, "novelists of manners," like Jane Austen, Maria Edgeworth, and Anthony Trollope, "never get below the crust of society." [116]

Scudder regards the work of Joseph Kirkland in much the same light, finding in Kirkland "not the realism of art, but the realism of nature," with a horizon "just as far as his eye can see, and no farther." Edward Eggleston, on the other hand, shows that "genuine interest in the great movements of human nature which lifts even a casual story . . . into dignity." "Whether they be realists or idealists," according to Scudder, writers must "set their bits of portraiture of human life in relation with the universal." Björnson, who "translated a Norwegian local life into an universal human one," offers an example. "According as one sees human life behind his eye or before his eye will the result be in his work," continues Scudder. He finds that Eggleston's book *The Graysons* is "a work of art and as such has a penetrating power, interprets life"; Kirkland's *The Mc-Veys,* in contrast, is only "a perishable photograph which may remind one of a phase of life but . . . has no power to reveal actual life." [117]

31

On the whole, it is Turgénieff who reveals life most satisfactorily to this group of critics. "A realist in the sense of hiding himself, and in the painstaking accuracy he shows with regard to everything his pen touches," [118] Turgénieff shows that further quality demanded by many *Atlantic* critics, "poetical insight." [119] And though they are happy to find in him "apparently great local truth" [120] and "life, nothing more, nothing less, though life altogether foreign to our own," [121] they are pleased, too, to find something more. As Lathrop points out, there are "the fresh, abruptly fractured surfaces of ordinary life together with the immeasurable depths of their suggestions." [122] Henry James, who finds Turgénieff's characters both "fascinatingly particular and yet so recognizably general," praises the Russian author for being "both an observer and a poet." [123] And whether the works be considered as "the intensest dramas of human passion, in which the old tragedy of hope, of despair, of love, of death, is played amid the shifting circumstances of everyday life" or as *"cultur romanen* which portray the intellectual and moral aspects of society," Clara Barnes Martin considers that "their highest merit comes from that clairvoyance of genius which sees in and through the traits which are most Russian, the larger outline, the broader movement, which makes all primarily human and universal." [124]

In fact, Turgénieff is the one author who seems to approach the standard which Perry sets up for the great novelist, that of bringing "to the treatment of the main questions of our existence a wide comprehension of their meaning and a sympathetic power of interpreting as well as narrating the events he imagines and puts before us." [125] Based always upon the materials of real life, his works, nevertheless, seem to avoid the dangers of the literalism that is precipitated, as Lathrop says elsewhere, whenever "the aesthetic balance between fact and idea is, from whatever cause at all, unsettled." [126]

That Turgénieff escapes the dangers of literalism is due in part to his imaginative insight into life. It is due also in part to his awareness of aesthetic principles. It is not only for his "wonderful knowledge of the human heart" that Perry praises him but also for his ability to write fiction that is "a work of art." [127] To Howells, *Smoke* is "morally and aesthetically . . . a fiction of the highest class." [128] Henry James expresses appreciation for Turgénieff's "combination of beauty and reality." [129] That the Russian novelist cared "to make his tales brief and shapely" [130] is, in fact, an important factor in his popularity with *Atlantic* critics.

For just as *Atlantic* criticism frequently takes exception to the position that mere accumulation of observed facts will achieve the desired literary effect, so it likewise takes exception to the view that any fact or any arrangement of facts is as good as any other. "We do not need to be reminded that art and nature are distinct," writes Charles Dudley Warner in an essay on "Modern Fiction" in 1883, "that art, though dependent on nature, is a separate creation. . . ." Using Scott's *The Heart of Midlothian* as an illustration, he points out that Scott's art had "shorn" the raw material of his story "of irrelevancies; magnified its effective and salient points; given events their proper perspective, and the whole picture due light and shade." [131]

Although Turgénieff perhaps meets artistic standards more fully than most of his contemporaries, there are others who observe aesthetic principles in their treatment of realistic material. Of Mary E. Wilkins, for instance, it is said that "her art lies in her selection," that her effect is achieved "without any sacrifice of essentials and by no mere narrowness of aim, but by holding steadily before the mind the central, vital idea to the exclusion of all by-thoughts." [132] Mary Noailles Murfree, likewise, depends upon selection and arrangement of materials, grouping them "to disclose their meaning, not to invest them with some adventitious force." [133] James Lane Allen, who is "not tempted by realistic effects in the ordinary sense," is praised for his "tact of omission" and for a selection which has "beauty as its end." In "Sister Dolorosa" Allen is said to achieve "harmony in the strict classic way" with the landscape becoming a "symbolism of the human problem rather than a local background." [134] And Charles T. Copeland, writing in 1893 of Jane Austen, "the best sort of realist before realism was yet a christom child," attributes to that author "the extremely rare gift of tracing faithfully through transparent pages the outlines of her world . . . filled in with an artistic discretion far enough removed from the photographic process which is scarcely more satisfactory when it succeeds than when it fails." [135]

For Horace Scudder there is a convenient illustration to be found in Henry James's short story "The Real Thing," one which serves well to mark the distinction between content, the actual, and what Mark Schorer has called "achieved content," or art. Noting the differences between the report of actual adventures and the invented story, Scudder writes, "Mr. Henry James, in one of the subtlest of his stories, 'The Real Thing,' has touched most firmly this interesting truth in art, that the actual is not by any means the real." [136] And in another review in the same year he turns again to the story for illustration of the creative faculty. "Why is it," he asks, "that the more perfectly a wax figure simulates life the more objectionable it becomes, the farthest removed from genuine life?" "What is there in art, literary or plastic," he continues, "which requires the making anew before we resign ourselves to entire satisfaction in what reflects our common humanity?"[137] To Mrs. Humphry Ward, who attempts "to transfer to her novel" the people "of the actual world in which she lives," he suggests the lesson learned by James's artist, a man who "thinks himself very fortunate in having a real lady and a real gentleman to act as models, but discovers before long that they may be real enough in actual life, yet are inferior models. . . ."[138]

According to Henry D. Sedgwick Jr., the artistic process which transforms facts into art may be described in terms of the feats of a juggler. As Sedgwick expresses it, "An artist takes a fact very much as a juggler does, holds it in his hands, makes a few quick movements, stretches it out to the beholder, and lo! the fact is entirely changed from what it had first seemed to be." This faculty of the artist, he continues, "has the power of throwing light on a subject, so that the humanly interesting element disentangles itself and stands out like the spirit of the fact, quite extricated from its trappings." He considers that "it is the lack of this faculty in both readers and writers that has brought philo-realism into passing fashion," that "has bestowed so much rash flattery upon this realism."[139]

The tone of Sedgwick's remark, very different from that of the excited response accorded to "truth" and to "accurate observation" by the early critics of realism reminds us that the pattern of reaction to that movement is not a simple one. Certainly the number of critics represented, as well as the length of the period under study, makes it dangerous to speak glibly of *Atlantic* criticism as an entity. But if we can hardly speak of any single pattern of that criticism, we can speak of several rather sharply defined trends. There is, as we have seen, very real praise for authors who attempt to offer, instead of the remote and etherialized locales of romanticism, actual and verifiable scenes. In fact, Howells' comment in 1876 on *The*

Adventures of Tom Sawyer—"fidelity to circumstance which loses no charm by being realistic in the highest degree, and which gives incomparably the best picture of life in that region as yet known to fiction" [140]—must be seen to stand for a consistent critical position which welcomes, and does much to promote, realism. To be sure, it is a position which for some time still bears traces of romanticism as indicated by the emphasis on local color and foreign "idylls." But it is a position which likewise does not ignore "the commonest occurrences of everyday life" [141] or fail to advise writers to portray everything "exactly as it is." [142]

Even critics who would make certain reservations about realism concede the value of this emphasis on real life. Paul Shorey, for instance, writes, "We may cordially admit that it is better to do what Miss Wilkins does for the life of the New England village, or Octave Thanet for the thriving towns of Iowa, or Mr. Fuller for the motley process which strives to keep up with the swift march of events that is converting the overgrown village of Chicago into the metropolis of a continent, or Mr. Cable for his Creoles, or Miss Murfree for her Tennessee mountaineers, than it would be to invent belated tales of chivalry or impossible adventures in fantastic Eldoradoes of unknown Africa." [143] And Harriet Preston comments, "If we weary sometimes of the incessant occupation of the realist with every-day types of characters, of the monotonous march of the action of his piece over the vast and melancholy levels of average experience, we must needs revere his universal sympathies, his indifference to outside show and vulgar celebrity, his patient study of the springs of action and unflagging researches into the dim secrets of the human soul." [144] That "the realistic novel has made it forever impossible that we should acquiesce in the violation of essential truth for literary effect" [145] is readily conceded.

Insistence on the actual does not mean, however, that for most of these critics representation of objective reality is to be equated with "truth" as presented by the artist. "There is an art we modern Americans need," states Christopher Cranch, a guest reviewer, in 1874, "and that is to go deeper than imitation,—to take nature as a base and scaffolding, but build thereon somewhat as the poets love to build." [146] Many of the regular *Atlantic* critics would agree with him. For to them it is not Trollope, the literalist, not Zola, the scientist, but Turgénieff, the artist, who truly deserves the name of "realist."

CHAPTER TWO

THE STRUCTURE OF THE REALISTIC NOVEL

OF NO OTHER GENRE CAN IT BE SAID AS TRULY AS OF THE NOVEL that, throughout much of its history, it has been a form without a form. "A literary mongrel" Joseph Warren Beach has called it, a term that recognizes its peculiar combination of drama, chronicle, and essay.[1] To W. L. Symonds, who in an article in the *Atlantic* in 1860 calls novels the "gypsies and Bohemians" of literature and finds their theme and treatment as "lawless as the conversation of an evening party,"[2] lawlessness appears as an advantage, in that it allows greater freedom to fiction. But *Atlantic* critics in general are not inclined to agree with him.

Thus George Parsons Lathrop in 1873 finds it an unhappy situation that "the English and American public of novel readers have, it would seem, a vague unwarrantable impression that the novel is but a careless, easy-going composition in which certain principles of dramatic writing may often with advantage be set aside and seldom need to be regarded."[3] Harriet Waters Preston expresses annoyance with writers—especially American women who produce novels—who seem to feel that any "once there was" story is worthy to be called a work of fiction. "A story, properly speaking," states Miss Preston, "is a thing of shape and boundaries and motive, not a portfolio of loose sketches, however charming, nor a rehearsal of long conversations, however natural and gay."[4] Horace Scudder, lamenting the fact that we seem to be "entering a period when almost everyone will write fiction," finds "little comfort for the few of us left to read and not write if we did not believe that grace of style, feats of invention, and cunning of construction would separate some of the productions and make them worth reading." [5]

Atlantic comments on the form of the novel are specific enough, however, to allow us to turn from this general dissatisfaction to more positive standards. Thus we find an earnest attempt to establish for the novel a structure that will replace the melodramatic plot of sensation writing, a form that will be based on the cause and effect logic of real life. There is a corresponding attempt to free the novel from those elements which tend to destroy the illusion of reality. And there is a steady insistence that the novel present its portrayal of life in dramatic form.

In some of the earliest reviews critics are still apparently seeking the traditional form of story which, through various exciting incidents, holds the reader's interest and offers him entertainment. The first novel reviewed in the *Atlantic,* Charles Reade's *White Lies,* is commended, for instance—despite its use of "artifices almost theatrical"—because of the author's "sure knowledge of the means and contrivances by which expectation is stimulated, and the interest of the story kept from flagging." [6]

As long as the story itself is the focus of interest, criteria are based on the skillful management of the story to lead to a *dénouement;* and though there is a demand for probability, such probability is based chiefly upon the relation of the events to the plot. "To secure the attention of his readers," writes F. H. Underwood in 1859, "the novelist must construct a plot and create the characters whose movements shall produce the designed catastrophe." [7] Similar insistence on the careful combination and succession of events, in terms of the designed catastrope which Underwood mentions, is suggested in the common complaint that "the faculty of making a well-constructed story, in which each event shall come in naturally, and yet bring us one step nearer to the journey's end, is now one of the lost arts of the earth."[8] E. P. Whipple's review of *El Furedis* in 1860 notes that "there is hardly anything in the book that can rightfully be called plot. The incidents are not combined...."[9]

Writing about James Fenimore Cooper in 1862, G. S. Hillard sets up a series of questions which may serve as a basis for critical judgments: "Are his stories, simply as stories, well told? Are his plots symmetrically constructed and harmoniously evolved? Are his incidents probable? and do they all help on the catastrophe? Does he reject all episodical matter which would clog the current of the narrative? Do his novels have unity of action? or are they merely a series of sketches, strung together without any relation of cause and effect?" "In works of fiction," he adds, "the skill of the writer is most conspicuously shown when the progress of the story is secured by natural and probable occurrences."[10]

Hillard's desire for natural and probable occurrences must be seen as part of the general reaction against the "romanticistic" elements of the melodramatists and the sensationists, "the broad canvas, the vivid colors, the abrupt contrast, and all the dramatic and startling effects that weekly fiction affords, the supernatural heroine, the more than mortal hero."[11] Such a reaction is to lead to a new interest in actual character and in action based on motives which may be recognized as true to life. Thus as early as 1858 it is noted that *The New Priest in Conception Bay* derives its interest "more from marked and careful delineation of individual character than from the march of events or brilliant procession of incidents."[12] A reviewer comments of George Eliot's *Scenes of Clerical Life* that "the public is learning that men and women are better than heroes and heroines, not only to live with but also to read of." [13]

The emphasis on life-like characters becomes so marked, in fact, that special care is taken to distinguish the novel from the romance, a form which gives less detailed delineations of character. For due credit can be given to such a writer as Nathaniel Hawthorne only by insisting, as does Howells, that "the romance and the novel are as distinct as the poem and the novel." [14] It is a distinction that Hawthorne himself had made in 1851 when, in claiming a certain latitude for his own writing, he had differentiated the romance from the novel, with its "minute fidelity, not merely to the possible, but to the probable and everyday course of man's experience." [15] Hawthorne's position is at no time denied in the *Atlantic*; indeed, he is now and then even compared with the Russian novelist Turgénieff for his treatment of the serious problems of existence.[16] Most contemporary *Atlantic* critics would agree with the opinion of James Russell Lowell, that "it is impossible to think of Hawthorne without at the same time thinking of the few great masters of imaginative composition." [17] E. P. Whipple, for instance, declares that "in intellect and imagination, in the faculty of discerning spirits and detecting laws, we doubt if any living novelist is his equal." [18] But both Whipple and Lowell make reservations about his characters. Whipple suggests that in Hawthorne "character is introduced, not as thinking, but as the illustration of thought," that his characters are "phantasmal symbols of a reflective and imaginative analysis of human passions and aspirations." [19] Lowell complains, "Helen we know, and Antigone, and Benedick, and Falstaff, and Miranda, and Parson Adams, and Major Pendennis—these people have walked on pavements or looked out of clubroom windows; but what are these idiosyncrasies into which Mr. Hawthorne has breathed a necromantic life, and which he has endowed with the forms and attributes of men?" [20]

Hawthorne's position, then, could be assured in part only by accepting his own distinctions between the novel and the romance. Thus Howells, defending Hawthorne's people against James's charge that they are "rather types than persons, rather conditions of mind than characters," states that it is "almost precisely the business of the romance to deal with types and mental conditions." [21] And this difference in standards is applied to certain other writers as well. "Character-painting is unessential to a romance, belonging as it does properly to the novel of actual life in which the romantic element is equally out of place," [22] writes Lowell in his review of *Sir Rohan's Ghost*. Howells deals leniently with Cherbuliez's *Joseph Noirel's Revenge* on the grounds that "the book is a romance, not a novel, and it would not be right to judge it by the strict rules of probability applicable to the novel." [23] And a review of "The Lady of Little Fishing" speaks of "that internal harmony which is the only allegiance to probability we can exact from romance." [24]

But whatever allowances might be made for the romance, it is not the romance, but the novel, which occupies chief attention. And the novel, in its accepted *Atlantic* definition, means realistic fiction. Such realism could be partially achieved, as we have seen, by giving close attention to objective details and to accurate portrayal of scene. But there is an even greater demand for accurate and careful portrayal of character. "The truer the 'local color' of the latter part of the book," writes Harriet Waters Preston of William Black's *Green Pastures and Piccadilly*, "the less it suits those ideal beings whom we find it so difficult to associate with the scenes portrayed." [25] Thus critical acclaim goes chiefly to authors whose characters are "like people in life." [26] "His soldiers are the soldiers we actually know," writes Howells of De Forest, "the green wood of the volunteer, the warped stuff of men torn from civilization and cast suddenly into the barbarism of camps, the hard, dry, tough, true fibre of the veterans that came out of the struggle." [27] George Eliot is likewise praised because her persons "show little sign of being 'rubbed down' or 'touched up and varnished' for effect." [28]

The emphasis on life-like characters leads in turn to a demand for plausible motivation of action. In a review of Wilkie Collins' *Armadale* in 1866 the necessary relationship between action and character is strongly emphasized. Stating that Collins' stories "are constructed upon a principle as false to art as it is to life," the critic writes, "In this world we have first men and women, with certain well-known good and evil passions, and these passions are the causes of all the events that happen in the world." "We doubt if it has occurred to any of our readers," he continues, "to see a set of circumstances, even of the most relentless and malignant description, grouping themselves about any human being without the agency of his own love or hate." The trouble with Collins' work is that the persons "are not to act out their own characters; they are to act out the plot; and the author's designs are accomplished in defiance of their several natures." Though the critic admits that the book has a kind of "verisimilitude," he finds the characters mere "puppets without proper will or motion." [29]

For works in which action proceeds from character, on the other hand, there is considerable praise. The critic of *Adam Bede* commends George Eliot in 1859 for her "general perception of those universal springs of action which control all society, the patient unfolding of those traits and humanity with which commonplace writers get out of temper and rudely dispense."[30] *The Mill on the Floss* shows "a far keener insight into human passion, a subtler analysis of motives and principles...."[31] The plot grew "naturally out of the characters,"[32] writes Howells in 1866 of Reade's *Griffith Gaunt*. Thomas Sergeant Perry notes that in *Babolain,* by Gustave Droz, the hero's troubles "are not thrust upon him . . . but they follow from his nature."[33] "A wonderful study of the way in which faults may be committed and of their natural punishment"[34] is Perry's comment on *Spring Floods* by Turgénieff. Henry James, in an early article on George Eliot, states, "I do not remember, in all her novels, an instance of gross misery of any kind not directly caused by the folly of the sufferer."[35] And Harriet Waters Preston finds in *Colonel Dunwoddie, Millionaire* a "real hero" whose character is so well drawn "that all his previous and all his subsequent career, every act, word, project, chimera, blunder, and triumph become logical, natural, and necessary."[36]

Attention to actions that "depend for their existence on the nature of the persons whose fate is described"[37] means, for the most part, the assumption that the individual determines his own fate. Occasionally, however, this strict insistence on personal responsibility is modified to include the "Fate" that is, for such a writer as George Eliot, "the compounded destiny of natural laws, character, and accident, which we call life."[38] Thus A. G. Sedgwick remarks of George Eliot's work, "It leaves nothing out of view; neither the material, nor the moral forces; neither the immutable fixity of physical succession nor the will."[39] But we are still a long way from any mechanistic determinism or from emphasis on chance, as Miss Preston's review of *The Return of the Native* indicates. Impressed though she is by the tragedy, which she describes as "simple, circumstantial, inevitable, never once . . . breaking down into melodrama," and by the whole movement of the characters as "the strenuously developed logical result of their circumstances," she does, however, suggest a "feeble suspicion of the freedom and accountability" of Hardy's characters.[40]

With the increase of interest in character and in causality of action comes a corresponding decrease in the attention paid to plot and story. Writing of Thackeray in 1870, Howells admits that the English author did not have a good knack of invention, but he adds, "what need had he of it, who could give us real men and women, and who could portray life so truly that we scarcely thought of asking about a plot?"[41] *The Luck of Roaring Camp* seems to Howells "rather weak" in plot, but he is quick to add that the world has outlived the "childish age in fiction, and will not value these exquisite pieces the less because they do not deal with the Thrilling and the Hair's breadth." He concludes, "People are growing, we hope, . . . to prefer character to situation and to enjoy the author's revelation of the former rather than his invention of the latter."[42] Perry refers in 1878 to *Chedayne of Kotono* as proof, "if any proof were needed at this point of the world's history, that a novel is not made interesting by the mere combination of unexpected and more or less tragic incidents." "What everyone cares for more than anything else," he writes, "is something like life in the characters, and this is totally wanting here."[43] And though Miss Preston announces that George Washington Cable —if he is to become capable of writing a full-length novel— needs to make use of the "old and much-discredited" plot, she is quite ready to say that such a plot "need not even be a matter of invention but only of watchfulness and memory." She adds, "The permutations and combinations of actual human life are infinite."[44]

Not plot, then, but a treatment of character which will leave the reader "with renewed amazement at the indissoluble connection between cause and effect" [45] becomes one of the most important of *Atlantic* criteria. In fact, George Parsons Lathrop writes in 1884 that the "greatest use" of fiction is "that of showing the process of cause and effect, through all of the incalculable diversities of individual experience." [46] And though Paul Shorey in a later article expresses certain reservations regarding realism, he concurs with that portion of the realist position which states that "the literature of the future must, in Emerson's phrase, deal with 'God's chancellors, cause and effect'; that it must represent things, persons, relations, and characters as grown-up men and women know them to be, and not as children and dreamers would fain make believe that they are." [47]

But the emphasis on "the real unity of development, sequence, and accident in human life" [48] is only one step in bringing the novel into closer correspondence with life. There remains, in addition to subject matter which is faithful to the patterns of life, the illusion of reality, an illusion that is often sacrificed in the traditional novel by the presence of the author himself. Novel writers who take their task lightly, who frankly tell their readers that this story is only make-believe, who lean back in their chairs and philosophize, or who comment on their characters, explaining what kind of people they are or why they are as they are, will soon sacrifice the sense of reality that has been gained by the subject matter itself. In addition to the demand for real characters and causal development of action, then, comes a demand for objective treatment, for the removal of the author from his own stage.

Objections to authorial comments are found early in *Atlantic* reviews. In 1858 James Russell Lowell finds that the author of *Beatrice Cenci* "interrupts his narrative too often with reflection and disquisition"; [49] in 1859 there is objection to a long financial discussion in Reade's *Love Me Little, Love Me Long*;[50] and another critic complains of the "intrusive little digressions in *Sword and Gown* "which everywhere appear, and which, jumping at random through passages of history, religion, art, politics, literature, as a circus-rider forsakes his steed to dash through the many-colored tissue screens that are held out to him," [51] interfere with the progress of the story. Harriet Preston's figure of "a sewing machine that skips stitches" [52] offers not a bad description of many of the novels of the day. And Howells' figure—that of a journey in an old-fashioned stagecoach, in which the travelers have to get out every now and then and help "to pry the vehicle out of the sloughs and miry places" [53]—is equally picturesque.

In fact, the subject is one which receives an unexpected amount of critical attention. Noting that Holmes's methods are "largely those of the essayist," Howells comments that this essay method is characteristic "of the whole English school in which the author permits himself to come forward and comment on the action and on things in general, and subjects the drama to himself." [54] Lathrop likewise calls attention to the "traditional devices" of the English novel as those in which the author comes forward in his own person. "Certain men of genius have triumphed in this method," writes Lathrop, "but it seems open to question whether their best achievements were ever greatly assisted by the particular feature alluded to. 'To bring his armchair down to the proscenium and chat with us,' as George Eliot describes it, was the weakest point in Fielding's crude mouldings of the novel; but his more accomplished successors have chosen to imitate the fault, sometimes directly, indirectly sometimes, and George Eliot as well as the rest." [55] To Lathrop, Fielding is too "fond of whipping in and out among his characters, in person . . . and with a sufficiently cheery and pleasant defiance of all criticism." Nor is Lathrop pleased that the English novelist frequently "dissected his *dramatis personae* in full view of the audience." [56]

Among the great English novelists, only Jane Austen, whose "creations are living people, not masks behind which the author soliloquizes or lectures," escapes criticism. "These novels are impersonal," writes one critic; "Miss Austen herself never appears." [57] In *Henry Esmond,* to be sure, where there is "no superfluous dissertation," Thackeray shows his ability to bring "characters before us with the least possible interference when he chooses to do so," [58] but this method was not his usual one. And though George Eliot's "intelligent and comprehensive sympathy," [59] her strong moral tendency, and her portrayal of real men and women have "put her on a pedestal" [60] for many readers, her "undue inclination to reflection and metaphysical digression" [61] causes frequent censure. Thus though Henry James admits that it is to the "union of keenest observation with the ripest reflection that her style owes its essential force," he is hardly satisfied with her "descriptive, discursive method of narration." [62] Perry remarks that in *Middlemarch* "every process of Dorothea's mind is painstakingly exposed and interpreted." [63] And he suggests that it is only George Eliot's genius which allows toleration for the "clumsy form" of her work.[64]

American writers are guilty of the same faults. According to Howells, Thomas Bailey Aldrich "cannot deny himself the pleasure of making witty and humorous remarks upon his action and his people," a custom which Howells considers a "vice," despite the sanction of English usage.[65] Sarah Orne Jewett has difficulty in making her characters "act for themselves." "At present," remarks Scudder, "they cling to her skirts and she leads them about with her." [66] Miss Murfree "too often obscures the climax by her own quiet reflection, instead of leaving it

Criticism of Fiction

to affect us by its own inherent strength." [67] And even Francis Marion Crawford, whose dramatic ability is usually extolled, is guilty, at times, of manipulating his characters, an indirect method of authorial interference. "The more human the novelist's figures are," says Scudder, "the more the reader instinctively resents a too subtle disposition of their actions and an attempt at adjusting nicely all their relations." [68]

Scudder's advice to Miss Jewett on how to achieve in her work "an individuality apart from the author" is to exchange "the form of study which permits her to be present during most of the action" for the method often used by Henry James. To have the story told by an assumed narrator, he feels, "might gradually strengthen her in an ability to conceive of a story which had its own beginning, middle, and end and was not taken as a desultory chapter of personal experience." [69] Howells likewise commends the use of the assumed narrator, calling it an "excellent device" that promotes a "more dramatic presentation." In certain cases, however, he finds that even Henry James has "a tendency to expatiate upon his characters too much and not trust his reader's perception enough." [70]

It is this psychological expatiation or analysis which is found to be a fault in many authors. To analyze carefully was essential; "without having analyzed" the author would "have nothing to unfold by the dramatic method." [71] But to perform that analysis in the sight of the reader was to invite censure by critics who believe that psychological analysis must be translated into action and dialogue. "This material should be employed out of sight, in the decoction of a rich vitality for the nourishment of the fictitious individuals, and its function should be hidden from the common eye," writes Lathrop. "Incorporated in their crude state with the body of the story," he adds, such materials "ultimately entrap the author, and leave him, as the novel develops, in the attitude of one who is committed to an opinion he cannot conceal; he comes to take sides with the so-called good people against the so-called bad." [72] Charles Dudley Warner grants that "the sacrifice of action to psychological evolution" is in some ways an advance in fiction. But he believes that the story is, nevertheless, the indispensable thing in the novel and that the analytic method too often destroys the illusion of that story. Warner's demand is for characters "so vividly presented in action and speech that we regard them as persons with whom we have real relations and not as bundles of traits and qualities." "We want to think that the characters in a story are real persons," he writes. "We cannot do this if we see the author set them up as if they were marionettes, and take them to pieces every few pages to show their inner structure and the machinery by which they are moved." [73]

The dangers of analysis are avoided by J. W. De Forest, who does not study psychology "with his characters and us before him, as many do, but proves his knowledge of it, so far as is necessary, by the growth of his characters and the acts of their lives." [74] Warner, in *A Little Journey in the World,* is said to adopt "the manner of the naturalist school instead of having recourse to that which is wearisome in its use of psychological analysis." "He has made this analysis for himself," writes Scudder, "but when he comes to illustrate the downfall of Margaret Debree, he gives the steps by which its course proceeded, not the steps by which the process was interpreted in his mind." [75] Less successful than these writers, however, is Mrs. A. D. Whitney in *Odd or Even.* Scudder suggests that he would find her work much more satisfying "if she would be content with such a view of her characters as did not turn their souls wholly inside out; if, by a wise selection from a throng of incidents, those only were taken which would enable the reader to spell out the destiny of the *dramatis personae;* and if she were not bound always to tell both the dream and the interpretation thereof." [76] To its critic in 1883 Frances Hodgson Burnett's *Through One Administration* would likewise have been a better book had Mrs. Burnett allowed "the interaction of the characters to take place more positively through the incidents of such society and had depended less upon their perpetual comment." [77]

Henry James occasionally receives similar criticism. Scudder, for instance, is willing to grant that in James we know what certain facts mean, but only because of esoteric knowledge that we have already received from the author.[78] Harriet Preston finds *The Europeans* "a series of situations imperfectly vivified by action." To her James seems so *spirituel* that he lacks the "sense," a term that she uses "metaphysically and with entire respect" to portray his characters adequately.[79] Perry calls *Confidence* "really not a novel but a study of an ingeniously devised situation that is analyzed and described with utmost skill." [80] And Scudder compares James somewhat unfavorably with Howells as he states that we know the latter's personages "in the same way we know the people whom we meet in actual life," without feeling ourselves guilty of any "conscious mutual analysis." [81]

In many of these reviews of the analytic novel it is not easy to separate the objections to analysis itself from those which are based upon a too intensive study of human nature or too great reliance on "minute touches." [82] Scudder writes of Constance Fenimore Woolson, for instance, that she is being led "farther and farther away from large pictures of human life into the windings and turnings of fictitious pathology." [83] That the novelist "retreats farther into the field of the human spirit, and plies his Roentgen rays to discover that which is hidden from observation" [84] is not always a pleasant prospect for the

Atlantic critic. "Our modern methods with their morbid cravings for individuality smack too much of the experimental psychologist," [85] observes one reviewer. And Hall Caine is characterized as "a moralist so possessed by the intricate errancies of the human conscience that he turns life into a pathological clinic." Few books, according to William P. Trent, offer "so melancholy an example of the tendency of current fiction to pathological excess" as Caine's *The Manxman,* "for here is a writer of normal healthy mind who cannot resist the temptation to follow his characters step by step through the inner chambers of their being, and to drag his readers along with him." [86]

Too often it would seem that the novelist "professes an intimate knowledge of the wheels, cogs, cranks of the brain, and of the airy portraiture of the mind . . . and describes them with an embellishment of scientific phrase, letting the outward acts take care of themselves as best they may." [87] Such a procedure seems fallacious to those *Atlantic* critics who insist that characters be presented in the novel, free from the laborious analysis of the author, and allowed to work out their own destinies. The higher art, according to Warner is "to treat them dramatically and let them work out their own characters according to their characters," [88] a criterion that allows for the three elements prominent in *Atlantic* comments on structure—freedom from authorial interference, a working out of character according to a cause and effect logic of motivation, and dramatic portrayal.

In insisting on dramatic portrayal, critics call attention to the drama inherent in the pattern of real life. " 'To observe minutely the several incidents which tend to the catastrophe or completion of the whole, and the minute causes whence these incidents are produced.' Here we have the root of dramatic development," [89] writes Lathrop. And Scudder, speaking in

1895 of Richard Harding Davis, comments, "Out of such a study [of human nature] comes a greater sense of the complexity of life, and out of this sense is born that conception of the dramatic meaning of life which underlies the successful construction of wholes in fiction." [90]

Lathrop offers truth as his justification for dramatic method, indicating that "in real life ultimate truth seldom finds a pure utterance." He writes, "In drama . . . we have a situation presented as nearly as possible (subject to aesthetic laws) in the way in which it would present itself in the fact; the involved truths of the whole proceeding being illustrated by the partial expressions of each individual, on his own behalf or in estimating his fellows; so that the final fleeting essence of the matter lies within the scope of inference only." [91] Thus he would seem to suggest that if the novel is to be true to life, it must adopt what might be called the dialectical process of life itself; and for Lathrop the closest approximation to this dialectical process is to be found in drama.

According to this assumption, "a resolute act of self-renunciation on the part of the author" is essential, not only because he "detracts from the realism of the story" whenever he "intervenes, visibly, between the reader and the characters of his story," but also because his reduction to "absolute statement" violates the truth that in life is discovered only inferentially. It is on this ground that Lathrop criticizes George Eliot's "overwrought completion" in *Middlemarch*, where he finds her people "elaborated almost to exhaustion." "By reducing everything to absolute statement and endeavoring to fix the final issues in penetrating and permanent phrases" the author cuts the reader off from the ability to make his own inferences. And Lathrop believes that "in proportion as dramatic skill is successful it stimulates in us the disposition and ability to make such inference." "As an effort of clear intellectual penetration into life," Lathrop would hardly ask for anything more successful than *Middlemarch,* but according to his demands for drama it is "too much of an effort . . . a study, rather than a finished dramatic representation." [92]

One of the first comments on dramatic portrayal is that of Charles Eliot Norton in his review of *Mademoiselle Mori*. "Not only are the characters distinctly presented," he writes, "but there is in them, what it is rare to find in the personages of our modern novelists, a real and natural development, which is exhibited not so much by what is said about them as by their own apparently unconscious words and acts." [93] It is a criterion to which Howells also frequently calls attention. In *The Story of Kennett* the author "forgets himself entirely in the book" and often manages "by a single incident to give sudden and important development to a character." [94] Auerbach's *Edelweiss* seems "to tell itself. From the beginning it *goes alone* and one does not think of the author until the end." [95] In *The Hoosier Schoolmaster* the characters "all have a movement of their own, too, which is something for characters." [96] *The Adventures of Tom Sawyer* is "very dramatically wrought." [97] Boyesen's *Gunnar*, tracing "the development of an artistic mind as it gropes upward through the narrow conditions of a peasant's life," offers a study that is "made dramatically, not analytically, so that it is a work of fine art." [98]

Lathrop commends Hardy's *The Hand of Ethelberta* because "everything is given in pictures so far as it may be," [99] and he writes of Mrs. Burnett's *That Lass o' Lowrie's* that "the characters, at least, evolve themselves in a purely dramatic way." [100] Harriet Waters Preston, finding that the characters in B. M. Butt's *Delicia* are "deftly balanced and discriminated, their destinies most naturally intertwined," states that "there is not a melodramatic situation in the book, hardly a dramatic one, one would say, until it is remembered how seldom the author speaks in her own person, how entirely and with what clearness the tale is told by the *dramatis personae*." [101]

It is Turgénieff, however, who offers the best illustrations of dramatic presentation. *Smoke* is called "a studiously simple record of what two persons said and did." [102] Lathrop notes Turgénieff's "fine artistic impartiality which enables his characters to stand apart from him and be themselves." [103] Howells speaks with praise of the lifelikeness and gradual revelation of character in *Dmitri Roudine*.[104] Perry approves the way in which the Russian author "merely sets before us, with exquisite skill, what had actually met his eyes," letting us see his characters "face to face and not merely telling us about them." [105] Turgénieff's method, which Perry characterizes as "picturesque, not analytical," [106] is further analyzed by Henry James, who notes that Turgénieff's works "give one the impression of life itself, and not an arrangement, a rechauffé of life." "His work," states James, "consists of the motions of a group of selected creatures which are not the result of a preconceived action but a consequence of the qualities of the actors." Instead of plot, which was "the last thing that he thought of," the Russian writer, according to James, was interested chiefly in "the figure of one individual or a combination of individuals whom he wished to see in action." "He always made them do things that showed them completely," [107] writes James.

That character, then, should not be "described, analyzed, or annotated," but "as in drama . . . revealed through action and dialogue" [108] appears as a consistent *Atlantic* standard, a standard which, by eliminating much of the essay element common in fiction, works toward a tightening of fictional structure. And there is also a demand by several of the critics for closer relations among "the several persons who constitute the cast." [109] Mary Noailles Murfree, for instance, is praised for the way that her characters "are conceived . . . not so much individually as in their relation to each other," with each used "to bring out the qualities of the other." [110]

There is a desire, likewise, for action toward some end. In fact, the term "story" is for Lathrop identified with the "series of precedences and consequences . . . toward which our most casual experiences shape themselves." Taking exception to "that disbelief in 'story' which Mr. James implies and Mr. Howells distinctly announces," he insists that the writer who "wishes to produce in fiction a large and responsive likeness of life" must be concerned not merely with "a given number of separate occurrences" but with the exhibition of "a train of incidents which shall repeat, with the closest possible adherence to actuality, the succession of affairs in our daily experiences." [111]

To critics who believe that "one purpose of art is to present that completeness which is only implied in the series," [112] a book which consists of separate "scenes rather than a connected story" [113] or which shows life "in a series of pictures rather than in a gliding panorama" [114] falls short of success. Scudder writes of William Waldorf Astor's *Valentino* that "it is a novel and we have a right to demand a certain concentration of interest, a culmination of movement, resulting from a constant direction of the mind toward this chief personage." [115] E. W. Howe's *The Story of a Country Town* seems merely a number of stories having "no real spinal column"; [116] in Keenan's *Trajan*, "instead of a story marching with cumulative effect to its close, there is a congeries of stories"; [117] in *The Cliff Dwellers*, since the treatment of the heroine is not adequate to allow her to link together the parts of the novel, there is merely "an aggregation of stories, with an elevator for the central column." [118]

In certain other works, however, the standard is illustrated positively. In *Tess of the D'Urbervilles* "the end is the logical goal of the steps of incident by which the story moves forward from the beginning." [119] In *The Romance of Dollard* the drama "moves forward with an acceleration of strength," for the author, Miss Catherwood, "is so dominated by her theme that every little incident falls into place with a prevision of the final event." [120] And Mary Noailles Murfree is praised for her "extraordinary faculty . . . for presenting successive *tableaux vivants*, and for so arranging the succession of these scenes that there is a moving narrative" and a culmination where "all the currents . . . meet by no melodramatic contrivance but by the impelling force resident in each." [121]

It is only the short story which these critics exempt from standards of movement and culmination. In the short story it is conceded that "space for the development of characters is wanting." "We accept characters made to hand," Scudder states, "and ask only that the occasion of the story be adequate." [122] It is conceded, too, that certain authors who lack the constructive power necessary for the novel may, nevertheless, succeed with the short story, which demands different abilities. Scudder writes that it is "scarcely to be expected that Miss Jewett will ever attain the constructive power which holds in the grasp a variety of complex activities and controls their energy, directing it to some exclusive end." But he suggests that she does have talents adapted to the short story, including the ability "to conceive a genuine situation, to illustrate it through varied characters, to illuminate it with humor and dewy pathos." [123]

Those critics who plead for movement toward a definite conclusion are opposing the assumption of many realists "that it is inartistic and untrue to nature to bring a novel to a definite consummation, and especially to end it happily."[124] Charles Dudley Warner, who calls this assumption "baseless," meets the arguments of those who say that "life is full of incompleteness" with the counter charge that it is "full also of endings, of the results in concrete action of completed drama."[125] Scudder, who believes that "the writer's business in telling a story is to make it a consistent whole,"[126] takes issue rather sharply with what he feels is the contemporaneous nature of Howells' position in *Criticism and Fiction*. He writes, "Art is the interpreter of nature, not its traducer, and in fiction as in all literature, he who sees wholes and not fragments is the master."[127] Thus he believes that "in a well-constructed novel, the characters move forward to a determination, and whatever intricacy of movement there may be, it is the conclusion which justifies the elaboration." He adds, "We are constantly criticizing, either openly or unconsciously, a theory of novel writing which makes any section of life to constitute a proper field for a finished work; however many sequels may be linked on, we instinctively demand that a novel shall contain within itself a definite conclusion of the matter presented to view."[128] To Lathrop there are "eternal laws of verity and falsehood, of justice and of what we name injustice; abiding designs of strength and beauty which it is the novelist's mission to indicate. . . ." And in these laws he sees "a very substantial basis" for stories with an "intelligible 'ending.'"[129]

It is because of his attention to drama, action, and story that Francis Marion Crawford wins the approval of Scudder and Lathrop. Scudder, for instance, finds the attraction of much of Crawford's work in its "really being a tale,"[130] one in which "something constantly happens."[131] And Lathrop, at least on one occasion, suggests that Crawford represents "the best sort of realism," "the realism of the future." "It is not cramped by fear of incident; it does not lose itself in a microscopic study of details; there is no morbid anatomizing about it, and no space is lost in discoursing upon the characters; these are simply placed before us with a bodily distinctness that cannot be evaded," [132] writes Lathrop. And though there is "an abundant paraphernalia of local details," they are all "subordinate to the main issue." [133] To Scudder, Crawford appears to have regard for "the fundamental canons of the art of fiction," for "he conceives his characters; he regards them in relation to one another and to an actual world; he selects—what true artist does not select; and his characters fit into and explain one another." [134] A realist in the sense that the actions in his fiction "spring from motives clearly apparent" and that "the issue is logical," [135] he avoids, however, excessive refinement or analysis. And thus he meets Scudder's preference for the novelist "who is true to the broad exhibition of nature, and contents himself with seeing in the persons of his drama what any person of high, but not diseased, intelligence can readily apprehend and follow, and then directs his attention to giving free play to his figures within normal lines of action. . . ." [136]

The comments on Crawford, as can readily be seen, are a re-statement of many of the principles of *Atlantic* criticism. It is a statement which early turns its attention from those plots in which persons were "cut out to fit their places in the piece" [137] to careful study of character. That the action must appear as necessary, as the inevitable result of the natures of the *dramatis personae* is strictly insisted upon. And that the *dramatis personae* fulfill their dramatic role in presenting their own story without authorial interference is equally important.

In fact, Charles Miner Thompson suggests in 1897 that the critic in making his judgment may find it useful to look upon a novel as if it were a play. "Looking upon the story with the eyes of the dramatist," he writes, "you will see all its imperfections fade away,—all the 'analysis of character,' all the author's wise or humorous reflections, all the episodical incidents." And he adds, "Everything by which writers of novels are enabled to blind their readers to the structural weakness of their production or to the essential improbability of their themes seems to detach itself and vanish, leaving the substance and form naked to the eye." [138]

Thompson's method would perhaps not be acceptable to all *Atlantic* critics, for it suggests a rather serious confusion of *genres*. But it does offer as concise a summary as we may wish of those practices which they find objectionable, and it does remind us of the place which considerations of form and structure occupy in *Atlantic* criticism during this period. It reminds us, too, that behind most of the pronouncements about structure lies the standard that "the fundamental aim of the great novelist" is "in character, and character dramatically presented." [139]

CHAPTER THREE

THE REALISTIC NOVEL AND SOCIETY

JUST AS REALISTIC STANDARDS IN THE ATLANTIC SHOW A direct influence on both the materials and the structure of the novel, so they also have bearing on the problem of the relation of the novel to society. In considering that relationship it is necessary to give attention to the *Atlantic*'s view of the serious purpose of fiction; to its opposition to didacticism, one of the most frequent forms of authorial interference; to the new problems of taste and propriety raised by extension of subject matter; to the growing tendency to include in fiction social, economic, and political issues; and to the author's attitude toward his materials, an issue brought to the front by the "scientific" approach of many realists.

The serious purpose of literature is announced in the *Atlantic* by its first editor, James Russell Lowell, who, in writing of Poe and Hawthorne, defines the difference between "talent carried to its ultimate" and "genius" on moral grounds, the difference "between a masterly adaptation of the world of sense and appearance to the purposes of Art, and a so thorough conception of the world of moral realities that Art becomes the interpreter of something profounder than herself."[1] To Thomas Sergeant Perry "the more serious the nature of the problem" that a piece of fiction discusses "the higher its position as a work of art." "What more need be asked of a novelist than that he draw men and women as they are, with their faults and virtues ever merging into one another, and that he put these people into such relations as arouse our sympathy for some of the most serious matters of human experience," [2] he writes. To Howells fiction should be "a just man's experience of men"; only thus can it escape "from being the weariness and derision of mature readers." [3]

"When the artist succeeds in carrying us sympathetically through the history of these beings, so that we feel points of similarity between ourselves and them and recognize how great are the possibilities of crime and error in us, as in them, he has quickened our morality by rousing a keener insight into ourselves," [4] states Lathrop. Warner finds the value of literature in "the enlargement of the mind to a conception of the life and development of the race, to a study of the motives of human action, to a comprehension of history; so that the mind is not simply enriched but becomes discriminating and able to estimate the value of events and opinions." [5] Scudder believes that the moral nature of literature demands, likewise, ethical criticism. He writes, "Literature in its two-fold relation to art and life demands criticism which is historic and ethic as well as aesthetic." [6]

Such a consideration for the ethical, in the sense that those who deal fictionally with life must deal also with its serious problems, is reflected in the judgments passed upon individual authors. It is not only the "artistic impartiality" but also the "deep moral earnestness" of Turgénieff, who is "profoundly serious in behalf of what is good and just, even when he appears most impassive in respect to his characters," [7] which wins approval. Howells says of *Smoke* that "morally and aesthetically it is a work of the highest class." [8] Harriet Waters Preston finds the work of the Russian novelist not only "sufficiently captivating as mere stories" but also "full, and over-full, of a strange moral excitement, and of vast revolutionary suggestions for the more philosophic student." [9] And a review in 1874 suggests that Turgénieff's name "the literary history of our century must inscribe, with that of Hawthorne, high above all others who have dealt with the problem of evil." [10]

George Eliot is likewise considered "a profound moralist," [11] and one critic places *The Mill on the Floss* above *Adam Bede* on ethical grounds, because it "suggests a mental and moral philosophy nobler in themselves and truer to humanity and religion." [12] Harriet Preston, speaking of George Eliot's "immense moral momentum," adds, "Only Hawthorne and once Mrs. Stowe, on this side the water, have shown anything approaching it; and are they not our greatest?" [13]

Yet despite this basic criterion of morality, there is also a consistent demand that the artist integrate his art and his morality. For though the critics whose work is represented here were inheritors of the New England tradition of morality, a tradition strengthened by the tendency of realism to treat life truthfully and seriously, they were not inheritors of the New England tendency to preach in literature. To them moral intrusions were as out of place in fiction as were direct analyses of character or any other direct authorial intrusion. "The peculiar efficacy of a novel lies in its gradual, concrete, and insensible instillations of wisdom," Lathrop writes. He would allow the author to give his readers here and there "a few golden grains of formulated wisdom; but in general the abstract truth which he has laboriously eliminated should pass through the substance of his book like some chemic which leaves no trace in the liquid that absorbs it, beyond an increased brilliancy and clearness." [14] It is not by direct criticism, in Lathrop's view, but "only through clear perceptions into the true quality of our common nature, excited by the artistically recounted history of certain beings possessed of that nature, that the foundations of morality are deepened and secured." The novelist must give up the purpose of reform and consider instead his art. "If he understands that," Lathrop writes, "and thoroughly, conscientiously possesses himself of his theme, it will be strange, indeed, if his representation of life, like life itself, should not involve in every turn and folding some real moral enlightenment." [15]

That an author should consider his art rather than any conscious moral purpose is likewise advocated by Howells and James. "It is not as a moralist that we have primarily to find fault with Mr. Reade," states Howells, "but as an artist, for his moral would have been good if his art had been true." [16] Henry James's review of *Around a Spring* by Gustave Droz gives an early statement of James's view on the morality inherent in realism. "His work . . . carries the interesting reflection that intelligent realism, in art, is sure to carry with it its own morality," says James. "Told in a vulgarly sentimental manner, the history of Mademoiselle Cibot might mean nothing at all; told in its hard material integrity, as our author tells it, it enforces a valuable truth." Droz, he believes, "will be unlikely ever to write a tale which will not project a certain moral deposit and leave the reader, after many broad smiles, in a musing mood." To James, "such is the effect of all really analytic work." [17]

But such a view was hardly a widely held one, as Howells indicates when he speaks of "the large class of readers who cannot understand the difference between artistic reluctance to enforce a lesson that ought to teach itself and callousness to the sins described." [18] Thus there was need for a good deal of critical opposition to didacticism. Sometimes it is a writer's attempt to set up a "mechanical morality" [19] which is criticized. Lathrop reminds such an author—Richardson furnishes one example—that "moral truth . . . is not best advanced in works of fiction by opening a strict debit and credit account, which shall leave the deserving and undeserving characters at quits, before the finis is written." [20] To draw in total black and white is "an artistic as well as an ethical error" in the eyes of Thomas Wentworth Higginson. He reminds Jean Ingelow of the remark made by Porson to Rogers, that "in drawing a villain, we should always furnish him with something that may seem to justify him to himself" and also recalls the same rule in Schiller's aesthetic writings.[21] According to another critic, didacticism seriously interferes with truthful, realistic presentation. "The trouble with highly moralized novels," he writes, "is apt to be that they are not pictures of human experience, but the experience of preternatural automata," with the author's "purpose to do good" often overcoming his "instinct to be true." [22] To Balzac goes praise for avoiding black and white treatment. "Though he detested the Revolution of July and the bourgeoisie yet he did not devote himself to painting this class of society in black colors without relief." [23]

Most frequently, however, the objection is to the author who "never trusts the reader to do any moralizing for himself." [24] Howells writes of F. H. Underwood's *Lord of Himself* that the author "sacrifices his narrative again and again to his own wish to say certain things and develop certain doctrines which might have been better preserved for a separate work." [25] And he makes similar objection to the "long monologues and colloquies on morals" in Henry Ward Beecher's *Norwood*. "The homilies and discourses and essays are intolerable for where they are rather than for what they are," [26] he writes. Scudder takes a similar position, stating that "in art . . . a humane or religious sentiment must possess a work; it must not interrupt it." In his view we may "expect a literary result noble and enduring" only when a writer "succeeds in so adjusting his ethical nature to his artistic that the one shall be thoroughly infused with the other." Thus he complains that in *Dr. Sevier* George Washington Cable "had not so mastered his theme that he was able to present it through a culminating process of persons and events." He warns that the novelist, unless he "esteem more highly the dramatic quality of his work," is in danger of "giving us tracts instead of great novels." [27]

In George Eliot, for whom the world, according to Henry James, was "the moral, the intellectual world," and for whom the novel "was not primarily a picture of life, capable of deriving a high value from its form, but a moralized fable," didacticism was likewise a fault. Though James is willing to admit that the author's philosophic temper "widened the area of her aesthetic structure," he adds that "the philosophic door is always open, on her stage, and we are aware that the somewhat cooling draught of ethical purpose draws across it." [28] "She philosophizes very sufficiently," states James's character Constantius in *"Daniel Deronda;* a Conversation," but she has come near spoiling an artist." [29] Perry writes of the "dead weight of ethical considerations, in George Eliot's later novels, over which morality hangs like a heavy pall." [30] And Agnes Repplier, having counted "the obnoxious word 'ethics' six times" in one paragraph of a review after the novelist's death, states rather bluntly, "That some of us endure George Eliot the teacher for the sake of George Eliot the story-teller is a truth too painful to be often put into words." [31]

Reviews of works which make a more satisfactory combination of ethical interest and art suggest the pattern desired by *Atlantic critics.* According to Horace Scudder, S. Weir Mitchell's *In War Time* reveals "Dr. Wendell's paltering with his conscience so that the moral is involved in the story but is as clear as noonday to the reader." "It is by such books," he continues, "that the novel may prove its right to the office of *censor morum,* while it continues to be an agreeable companion; for we doubt if any homily upon honesty could be more effective than this perfectly natural portraiture of a weak man." [32] Perry makes similar comments on *Les Rois en Exil* by Alphonse Daudet. He notes that "without sermonizing, without contempt for the poor king, he has written what is a serious defense of upright conduct, simply by showing a weak, vicious man, and the consequences of his faults." He calls the book "a direct study from life" in which the "democratic feeling and this tone of moral earnestness were probably not intended to be prominent." Yet he believes that "it is their apparent subordination and real prominence that raise the novel from the rank of entertaining books to that of a really important one." [33]

But realism brought new problems, of taste if not of morality, in extending its subject matter to include areas of life sometimes closed to fiction. It could not be pretended, of course, that romanticism had treated only the good and the pure. The "long train of bigamists, murderesses, adulteresses, and dubiosities" which "the lady novelists on both sides of the Atlantic" [34] have added to literature receive Howells' censure in 1871. "The destroying military-man rides his usual course through these pages and breaks the heroine's heart; the baddish, beautiful woman flirts up to the brink of ruin, and tearfully retires upon the desolation of her husband," [35] writes another critic. An article on Disraeli suggests that that novelist's works hardly belong to "the fashionable school of fiction . . . since marriage vows are not broken in them, young girls are not depicted as monsters of vice, and the unrestrained profligacy of both sexes is not held up to the reader as the summit of human felicity." [36] And Perry comments that many of the sensation writers "exercise their invention merely in putting together all kinds of offensiveness." [37]

On the whole, the sensationists of whom Perry speaks receive relatively little attention. Thus Howells' question of whether morality and taste are a matter of subject or of manner[38] is more frequently asked in regard to the realistic fiction of the day. In general, extension of subject matter to include the less pleasant sides of life gives little trouble when only the works of English, American, or Russian writers are considered. Howells finds that Judd's *Margaret* is "marvelously, almost matchlessly frank in dealing with the rude life in which its scenes are laid" and adds that the author "no more moralizes that life or is ashamed of it than the sunshine would have been." [39] Clarence Gordon reports that *Miss Ravenel's Conversion from Secession to Loyalty* is "too honest to shirk the truth from conventional delicacy", but discovers "no coarse impression, result, or example." [40] "The artist who so represents vulgar life that I am more in love with my kind, the satirist who so depicts vice and villainy that I am strengthened in my moral fibre has vindicated his choice of material," writes Charles Dudley Warner. He does object, however, to treatment which pictures merely "the shady and seamy side" of life and leaves "the whole weltering mass in a chaos without conclusion and possible issue." [41] Scudder makes an occasional protest about Bret Harte's "unmoral treatment of immoral subjects," suggesting that "as soon as we fairly leave our conscience, like our coat, hanging on a nail outside and enter Mr. Harte's world in social and moral *deshabille*, we are entertained beyond measure." But his chief objection to Harte is based on that author's sentimentality of treatment; Scudder notes such a "complete . . . ascendancy of sentiment that there is a needless waste of morals." [42] Not subject matter, but treatment, is likewise the basis of criticism in Scudder's review of *The Story of a Country Town,* a book which has "no clear moral." [43] For James Lane Allen, who "uses the frankness of naturalism only that he may invest it with a forgotten reverence," [44] there is nothing but praise.

Lathrop at one point questions whether Turgénieff's "determined realism does not sometimes carry him too far in the treatment of passages which will hardly bear such treatment, however pure the artist's motive, without becoming a little more acceptable to the vicious than the virtuous." [45] And Whipple is thinking of "the verbal proprieties demanded by modern taste" when he speaks of Dickens' skill in portraying his characters "in their hideous reality" while denying them their "favorite outlets of expression in ribaldry and blasphemy." [46] But there is not likely to be much dissatisfaction if the material is treated in such a manner that the reader "bestows his pity and scorn in the right quarters and . . . perceives that the author is one with him in the judgment he passes." [47] For it is chiefly fiction in which the author's position is not made clear—though this must be done within aesthetic laws and not directly—which arouses disapproval.

There is at least a hint, however, that that ethical position must be one in which will plays a larger part than circumstance. "Fate is allowed an undue predominance over human will," [48] writes C. T. Copeland of Hardy's *Tess of the D'Urbervilles*. Scudder's review of *A Wheel of Fire* by Arlo Bates objects to the playing down of "spiritual sense" in favor of "physical weakness," of crowning "necessity instead of free will." Scudder writes, "We cry out against that 'must.' We refuse to accept a logic based solely on physical processes. . . . Reason, not unreason, lies at the core of life, and a picture which denies this is false." [49]

The stand which *Atlantic* critics find most palatable is expressed in Lida Krockow's comments on Hermann Sudermann, for she suggests that if Sudermann's characters "have human weaknesses, they possess at the same time firm and healthy fibres of will." And though "his pages teem with sins and small miseries . . . his characters make progress if not in material wealth, then in possession of character, insight, will, charity." [50]

French literature, however, is the focus for a number of attacks on immorality and lack of taste, for, according to Perry, "since 1830 the general course of the best French writers had been towards popular discussion of all sorts of matters which are not to be decided by the literary sense alone." [51] And not only do French writers overstep the boundaries of taste and morals; they justify their actions on the ground of art for art's sake. With such justification Perry has no patience, stating, "If it is not in the province of literature to teach morality, it also does not belong to it to teach immorality; but it is only the first division of this sentence which is denied by critics who plume themselves on their liberality." [52] Calling Zola's *L'Assommoir* an "outrage on decency," Perry writes: "It is singular how those who carry on the fight in defense of what they call art for art's sake, while they are discussing the theory, fly to lofty heights of abstract reason, but as soon as they come to put their reasoning into practice drop down to the sewers to lug something forth to astound the world." He is willing to concede that merit is to be found in the position in so far as it is a reaction "against a narrow, hypercritical intermeddling of the outside public. . . . " But those who would make it represent the full view of the case fail "as utterly as would those who should ask for a commission of clergymen, lawyers, merchants, sailors, and farmers to decide on the merits of a book before publication." [53]

Nor is Perry more in sympathy with the scientific aims of Zola and his followers who are "vying with each other in diving for material into the indescribable." [54] "It will be a fortunate day for art, and for the novel in particular, when the French shall have finished their exhaustive labors in the sewer and reached the level of the pavements," writes Sophia Kirk, warning the reader of Daudet's *L'Immortel* that he who enters "its Augean precincts will do so at his own risk and peril." [55] Perry agrees that "there are a great many things in nature which cannot be told, however truly." To him the place for treating sin, misery, and physical repulsion is in books of social science and political economy, not in novels. *L'Assommoir* "demands attention on account of its shameless assault on every principle of literature which distinguishes a novel as a work of art from a criminal indictment." [56]

Nor can Zola, for all his protests, be said to be really scientific; he is, rather, unscientific and inexact in "overlooking whatever is honorable in human nature." To the French novelist men and women are really beasts, and his heroes might better be described by the term "pathological" than by Zola's own word "physiological." [57] Of *Nana* Perry writes that "a book more redolent of corruption it would be difficult to find; it reeks with every kind of beastly sin." "Irredeemably vulgar" is his characterization of the author, who is "guilty of cramming his books with scandal." [58]

In drawing his support from Claude Bernard, Zola "overlooks one possible analogy" with the science of medicine, according to Perry. "He says nothing about the fact that medicine has for its sole object the cure of bodies, and that if literature is like medicine it must concern itself with the cure of men's morals," the critic writes. Perry would deny that literature is like medicine, or any other science, but he does believe that "what novels can do and novels have done is to affect men's opinions on a great many important questions." [59] The influence that novels can have on men's emotions is illustrated, he suggests, by such books as *Uncle Tom's Cabin,* Turgénieff's *A Sportsman's Sketches,* and Tourgée's *A Fool's Errand.*[60]

Perry's comments on Zola ignore that author's social purpose of exposing evils so that evils may be cured, but they do lead to another important critical problem, that of the treatment of social problems in fiction. That novels, though dealing with facts, do affect men's emotions and attitudes is generally accepted by *Atlantic* critics. That an author striving to portray life accurately may find legitimate materials in social, economic, and political issues is likewise granted. But just as morality must be an unobtrusive factor, so must social considerations find their place within aesthetic limits.

As early as 1864 Bayard Taylor's *Hannah Thurston,* which deals with the question of women's rights, is called "an able pioneer" both in subject and treatment, though the reviewer suggests that the treatment leaves something to be desired.[61] Howells, praising *Miss Ravenel's Conversion from Secession to Loyalty,* which deals with the issues of slavery, writes that "Mr. De Forest gains an immense advantage in refusing to deal with slavery except as a social fact." [62] Turgénieff's appeal is due in some measure to his dealing with the Russian problems of the day. "The keenness with which the leading Russian writers follow up the predominant faults of their countrymen is proof of considerable intellectual activity of a kind that observation teaches us is surest to bring forth good fruit," [63] writes Perry. But let even Turgénieff fail to integrate his materials and there is sure to be complaint. Thus Perry remarks that in *Terres Vièrges* "it is as if for once the author had harnessed together two uncongenial horses, information and entertainment." In *Fathers and Sons,* on the other hand, the character Bazaroff "keeps his proper place in the novel as a novel." [64]

The Realistic Novel and Society

This insistence that social issues be handled within the bounds of aesthetic principles is a constant one. James Russell Lowell, writing of *Miss Gilbert's Career* by J. G. Holland, suggests that "there is scarcely a more hazardous experiment for any novelist than a 'novel with a purpose,'" for in such books "if the moral does not run away with the story, it is in most cases only because the author's lucky star has made the moral too feeble."[65] Often it is the patches of propagandistic discussion which receive the same criticism as the other essay elements which we have already considered. "If those pages of endless moral labels could be cut out bodily," writes Ralph Keeler in a review of Spielhagen's *Hammer and Anvil,* "the reader ... might enjoy the pleasant but delusive impression that he had met that *rara avis* of the present literary period, a novel without a purpose."[66] Scudder, in reviewing *Hope Mills,* complains of the "endless detail, which is unessential to a story, however much it may be of service in a cooperative tract."[67] Too much "fragmentary and futile discussion of the temperance question" mars Jean Ingelow's *Sarah de Berenger;*[68] there are "too many diatribes and digressions" in *Baby Rue.*[69]

Helen Campbell's *Unto the Third and Fourth Generations* has faults which "appear to follow in part from the author's attempt at making the theory carry the story instead of the story carry the theory."[70] When theory becomes partisanship, similar aesthetic errors may occur. To Perry, reviewing Daudet's *Jack,* it seems that "the writer who is especially interested in setting some particular wrong right, or in branding it with hot contempt, is likely to let the precise development of his story and of his characters be neglected in his anxiety to make on the reader an impression as deep as that which he himself feels."[71] Such one-sided treatment may likewise result in a falsified picture of society. Lathrop finds De Forest's "intention in entering the field of social and political satire" to be "thoroughly good," but he questions the author's wisdom in treating merely the vulgar phases of society without giving pictures, as well, of something better. In Lathrop's view "there is something so shameless, defiant, and unpicturesque" about these crude phases of political life that "they must be treated cautiously, in glimpses only; or if broadly exhibited, they should be accompanied by redress in the form of pictures of something better." "This is certainly essential to an artistic result," he adds, and "probably it is so to the moral effect as well." [72]

During the 1880's the increase in the popularity of social and political novels is reflected in the greater number of reviews dealing with such themes. With the extension of the novel to politics *Atlantic* criticism is, on the whole, sympathetic. In Scudder's opinion, "There is no reason in the nature of things why a novel may not be a very truthful and very cogent political argument, since man is a political animal, and the novel excludes nothing which concerns the essential elements of human society." But he adds firmly that the novelist's business is "to state things as they are, not to plead a case." [73] Comments on *A Fool's Errand* and *Bricks Without Straw* illustrate his views of the difference between legitimate and faulty treatment of social problems. The former, which "commended itself by its freedom from partisanship," was always ready, "even with its recital of gross outrages," to give "an explanation which was not an exculpation but a reference back to historic causes and transmitted character," he writes. On the other hand, he considers that *Bricks Without Straw* "enters the arena as a somewhat angry and impatient officer of justice" instead of contenting itself with "a compact and well-studied statement in fictitious form of a great subject." [74] The tendency to become a tract is, however, perhaps the chief danger in such novels. In 1895

Scudder writes simply, "Being so excellent a tract, *Peter Sterling* is, naturally, not a particularly good story." [75]

Lathrop relates the treatment of social and political problems to the larger issues of aesthetic interpretation and definition. He grants that "there is no doubt a legitimate and extensive field for the novel in the political life of this country as related to other phases of human action and feeling." But he also insists that "it will never become incorporated with the domain of art until the belief has been abandoned that a mere lumping together of material, with no more integration or meaning than satisfies newspaper reporters, will produce a genuine novel." [76]

Scudder is especially concerned about the permanence of literature, a quality that can hardly be achieved without artistic treatment. He feels that often "the novel has become, like the daily newspaper, a record of the most recent facts in human history" and that "the novelists make haste to set down what people are talking about, before the people who talk have reached the end of their conversation." [77] "Say what we will about the novel as an engine of thought, or an instrument of torture, its primary end is as a creation on which its writer may look with satisfaction and say that it is good," he writes. Reminding his readers that "permanence is one of the attributes of a work of literary art," he continues, "When an author deliberately uses fiction to accomplish certain results, it is clear that when the occasion passes the use of the book has departed." [78]

Mrs. Humphry Ward, who is the subject of this criticism, is further censured for being "more interested in the effect of her novel upon certain minds than she was in producing a perfect work of art." [79] Though she appears to perceive "that fiction is not a vehicle for opinion," she seems unable, however, to "care for any persons whom she might create unless they were elaborately representative of opinions, and all actors in the drama of reform." [80] "A victim of the *Zeitgeist,* that scourge or that stimulant of literature, as one may choose to call it," is Scudder's characterization of her in another review as he adds, "Social reform, women, politics, the relation of man and woman in the apparent readjustment of society, here is double, double, toil and trouble, and Mrs. Ward puts her fagots on the fire and watches the cauldron bubble." [81] Charles T. Copeland, who writes that "every novel with a purpose except *Don Quixote,*—if indeed Cervantes seriously meant to smile 'Spain's chivalry away,'—has faded and withered in a surprisingly short time," grants that Mrs. Ward "ought to be given freely the palm for managing a novel of purpose better than anyone else has done." But he reminds her that "the working armament of polemics is impedimenta in art." [82]

Occasionally a writer is found whose work achieves a more satisfactory integration between art and social purpose. Scudder, for instance, finds considerable pleasure in Helen Hunt Jackson's *Ramona* because it "never loses its balance to become a plea." "On the contrary," he writes, "the artistic conception is so firmly held that the wrongs suffered by the Indians envelope and inclose Allessandro and Ramona as some dire fate, and though the reader is moved to indignation, his interest is never withdrawn from the story. The result is that the wrongs sink deeper into the mind than if they had been the subject of the most eloquent diatribe." [83] Jessie Fothergill's *Probation* offers an equally satisfactory treatment of a different kind of social problem. Scudder believes that "the distress and trouble of the Lancashire spinners are used legitimately, not to intensify our interest in the characters by the introduction of a bit of realism, but because characters and scenes all seem equally a part of the history." Instead of "abstract discussion of the relations of master and workman the reader is treated to something better in the relation of real persons to one another." "Out of the whole story," Scudder concludes, "one may gather some sensible reflections upon one phase of modern society." [84]

Reviews of the work of William Dean Howells allow us to trace somewhat more fully the stand taken by the *Atlantic*, during these years, on this issue of critical realism. Scudder, who is responsible for much of the criticism of Howells' fiction, approves Howells' turn in *A Modern Instance* to serious problems, writing that "it is the equilibrium of ethical and artistic powers which gives the greatest momentum to literature." For the moment he is apparently satisfied both by Howells' subject matter and his treatment, for he finds the book not "a tract" or "a plea" but "a demonstration of a state of society in which divorce laws are the index." [85] Yet in later reviews he seems to modify this view, for in 1885 he suggests that in *A Modern Instance* Howells' "habit of fine discrimination misled him into giving too much value in his art to the moral intention and too little to the overt act." [86] The following year he suggests that Howells "came alarmingly near giving his views upon the divorce question but was restrained by his artistic conscience and gave us instead the reflection of the surface without his own reflections upon the surface." [87]

His review of *A Woman's Reason* asks rather bluntly "if enough light has been cast upon a social problem to compensate for the loss of a piece of higher art." [88] *The Rise of Silas Lapham*, however, receives full praise as "a capital example of the difference between the permanent and the transient in art," a difference that arises from "the bottoming of art on ethical foundations." [89] In *A Hazard of New Fortunes* Howells "seems to have come near adjusting the ethical and aesthetic glasses with which he views life, so that they have the same focus." Scudder suggests that Howells needs "a large canvas and an abundance of material to serve as a check both upon his settled habit of using minute touches and his somewhat unsystematized discontent with contemporaneous society." He has learned, according to Scudder, that he "must select a few men and women, that they must have something to do with each other; that they must be a society within a larger whole." Under these circumstances he can let his people "play their own trifling comedies without detaching them from actual contact with the real world in which they were living." [90]

But Howells is not always found to be fortunate in his handling of social issues. Of *The Quality of Mercy* Scudder writes: "The book is so inferior to *A Hazard of New Fortunes* in respect to its characterization and play of persons that we have taken a little alarm lest Mr. Howells should have been misled by his subject, and be in danger of overvaluing what may be called the essay element in fiction." Stating that "we doubt if a novel has justified itself fully when its persons fade from the mind of the reader, and a few abstract principles remain as his chief possession," he continues, "Paulo-post future predictions are a crude form of criticism, but to say that a book of today will not be read by our descendants is to make an effort to detach the accidental circumstances from the essential art." [91] Harriet Preston, reviewing *An Open-Eyed Conspiracy*, suggests that Howells "has been so anxiously and almost morbidly preoccupied with American types and social portents and problems that it is pleasant to find him . . . dropping into something like the gay and engaging manner of former days." [92]

But to Sophia Kirk there is cause for pleasure in Howells' progress from a realism of "method" to a realism of "conviction." For her "the high water mark" of his fiction is reached in *The Minister's Charge* and *Annie Kilburn*—"where altruism has become an interpretative faculty"—and in *A Hazard of New*

Fortunes. "A close relation to the real brings a deepened perception of pain and discord, and an inevitable sense of 'the pity of it,' " she writes. And she adds that the author is "making us see America more truly, by bringing out its light and shade, by exposing its evil and good; it is by his sincere delineation—which is at the same time an interpretation—of America and human life that Mr. Howells points the way toward that comprehension and justice which lie on the attainable side of Altruria." [93]

The sense of humanity which Miss Kirk sees in Howells' later work raises another issue which occupies considerable space in *Atlantic* criticism. For some realists "the sacredness of the real" [94] meant, as for Howells, an increased social responsibility. For others, to whom realism was chiefly a method, it meant instead a "scientific indifference" [95] which many *Atlantic* critics could not condone. Writing that "the scientific motive is the predominant one," Lathrop complains that "our fiction writers become minute and sectional investigators . . . in search of specimens," that they "set them before us, connected by some slight story, and laugh and sneer at them a little, as if this were the extent of their obligation. . . ." He pleads for "a more reverent view of human nature, for without this nothing constructive can be done in art." [96]

Perry agrees with Lathrop, for to Perry scientific detachment succeeds in producing little more than "rather cold-blooded" [97] studies which appeal only to the intellect. "If the woman, and not the collection of things to say of her, were the main object of the story," he writes of Flaubert's "A Simple Heart," "the reader would feel differently about it." [98] According to Eugene Benson, Stendhal's work has "the interest of a dissection" and the author himself "the intelligence of a reporter, but not a heart that suffers and rejoices." [99] Cherbuliez's position is called that "of the scientific man rather than that of the poet, who laughs and cries and hates as may be required, without contenting himself with the chilly enjoyment of perceiving alone." In Turgénieff, on the other hand, "we feel the strong passion inspiring him and glow in sympathy." [100]

A similar detachment from life and humanity is the basis for much of the criticism of Henry James. Lathrop remarks that in *The American* James has approached "nearer to an air of simple human fellowship," [101] but other critics often agree with Harriet Preston's comment that to read James "is to experience a light but continuous gratification of mind. It is to be intellectually tickled, provided one is capable of such an exercise." [102] Perry suggests that the characters in *Confidence* "are a set of life-like figures, whose positions in regard to one another are distinctly drawn, and watching their movements is like looking at a well-played game of chess." [103] Scudder admits that *Washington Square* "is witty and sometimes ingenious" but he finds that the characters are "elaborate non-entities." [104] The characters of *The Portrait of a Lady* are "all true to the law of their own being, but that law runs parallel with the law that governs life instead of being identical with it." [105] And Scudder writes of *The Bostonians*, "Mr. James is bound to find out all he can about his characters, and he performs a vast number of experiments with them, extremely ingenious and very satisfactory to the scientific mind." [106]

For *The Tragic Muse,* however, Scudder has considerable praise, recommending it as "the facile instrument of a master who is thinking of the soul of his art." In fact, his review sets forth what may be considered a central *Atlantic* position. Stating that "the artistic defect of novels of purpose is that the function of the novel as a representation of life is blurred by the function of the tract," and that "the artistic defect in the novel without a purpose lies in the superficial dexterity which supposes life itself to be shallow and incapable of anything more than a surface gleam," Scudder concludes, "It is in the nice portrayal of surfaces, by which an undercurrent of moving life is now revealed, now concealed, that the highest art is disclosed." [107]

Most *Atlantic* critics would agree with Scudder, as they would also agree with Charles Dudley Warner, that the novelist must "reveal the real heart and character of this passing show of life." [108] They would subscribe to Agnes Repplier's view that "a transparently didactic purpose is fatal to the perfection of any work claiming to spring from the imagination." They would accept also that essayist's dictum that to overstep certain notions of decency is "an offense against art, for there is nothing so hopelessly inartistic as to represent the world as worse than it is." [109] They would grant that, since man is a social and political being, the novel may well deal with social issues, if those issues are submitted to the laws of art. They would ask that the writer exhibit artistic impartiality, but they would also ask that he show the artistic sympathy and interpretation which are necessary to a revealing of life in fiction. Perhaps the most serious charge that can be brought against this portion of *Atlantic* criticism is its middle of the road quality, its tendency to qualify many of its pronouncements. But it must be conceded that it not only maintains aesthetic standards in the face of both didacticism and propaganda but also helps to dignify the novel as a literary form by affirming its serious nature.

CHAPTER FOUR

SOME CONCLUSIONS

THAT REALISM SUPPLIES THE CHIEF "FIGURE IN THE CARPET" OF *Atlantic* fictional theory during the years just considered seems evident. That the figure is a complex one, ranging from enthusiastic acceptance and promotion of realism in certain of its aspects to rejection or modification of it in certain other phases is equally apparent. And that the figure is a more pervasive one than has perhaps been realized, affecting alike the subject matter, the structure, and the purpose of fiction must also be noted.

It is a pattern, as we have seen, which places emphasis on observation of actual localities and customs—with "truth" and "reality" serving as common critical counters for the appraisal of such early realists as John Townsend Trowbridge, Theodore Winthrop, and J. W. De Forest. Delighting in the slightly romanticized reality found in sketches of the recent past and of little known sections of America, it gives critical support to local colorists like Sarah Orne Jewett, Mary Noailles Murfree, Bret Harte, and George Washington Cable. It brings to the attention of American readers the simple, idyllic stories of Björnson, Auerbach, and Boyesen. And it gives due credit to Victor Cherbuliez, Gustave Droz, Daudet, and even to Zola for making use of actual, concrete detail and thus helping to turn fiction to a consideration of real life.

85

It insists on truth of character portrayal, requiring both the presentation in fiction of ordinary men and women and a strict sense of motivation, criteria illustrated in the novels of George Eliot and Ivan Turgénieff. It seeks not only reality in subject matter but an additional reality of method, for according to its standards no novel can appear real if the author steps at will upon his own stage to offer philosophic comment or to discuss openly the psychological processes of his characters. Thus it demands withdrawal of the author in his own person and the presentation of the story through the action of the characters themselves. In accord with its view of the cause and effect sequence of human life, it asks that this dramatic presentation have a tighter structure than that of either the sensation novel or the novel of manners.

The desire for an illusion of reality to be gained by the removal of the intrusive author results in constant objection to overt moralizing, even in a novelist otherwise as much admired as George Eliot. But despite the opposition to didacticism, the pattern is one which places upon the novelist the obligation of insight into the most significant problems of human existence, a position deriving basically perhaps from the New England tradition of morality but intensified by the new tendency to view fiction as closely associated with life. It includes treatment of social and political issues, provided that the treatment be within the limits of art.

For aesthetic standards serve as a constant corrective for those who would blur the distinction between actual reality and the reality seen by the artist, for those who would allow the novelist to be a reporter rather than an artist. And it is against the standard of the artist, whose imaginative insight puts a meaning beween the lines of his representation and gives definition and conclusion to his picture of life, that the work of a literalist like Trollope, of a detached observer like Cherbuliez, or of an avowedly scientific writer like Zola is judged.

With such a general framework as background it becomes possible to note certain individual differences among the critics represented. For though such differences can hardly be said to change the general pattern of *Atlantic* criticism, mention of them will allow us to focus attention on critics like Lathrop and Scudder, whose work has not yet received separate study. And it will likewise allow us to draw certain comparisons between their work and that of Howells.

A major portion of the critical writing on fiction during the period was the work of five critics—Howells, Perry, Lathrop, Scudder, and Harriet Waters Preston. Approximately sixty-five of the pieces on fiction are by Howells, forty by Lathrop, one hundred by Perry, one hundred by Miss Preston, and nearly two hundred by Scudder. Perhaps little distinction can be claimed for the work of Miss Preston, for though Howells seems to have turned over much of the reviewing to her during 1878 and 1879, many of the books which she notices at that time are decidedly third-rate. Nor do her reviews of other novels show any special critical insights. Perry's criticism has already been the subject of study.[1] But a word should certainly be said about Lathrop, whose two long essays on the novel in 1874 are among the best critical writing that appears in the *Atlantic* during this period, and about Horace Scudder, who from 1880 until 1898 is responsible for much of the *Atlantic* comment on fiction.

Howells and Lathrop may be said to be united in their demands for accurate portrayal of life, in their interest in character and their desire for a dramatic presentation of that character according to a cause and effect sequence, in their dislike for the intrusive author, and in their belief that the moral effect of a novel must be produced indirectly. But on the issue of what Lathrop calls literalism there is at least a difference in emphasis. To call it more than a difference in emphasis would, I think, be false, for it is possible to find in Howells' reviews sentences that might have been written by Lathrop. For instance, Howells writes of Sarah Orne Jewett's *Deephaven,* "We are very glad of these studies, so refined, so simple, so exquisitely imbued with a true feeling for the ideal within the real." [2] He suggests that Björnson is "the reverse of all that is Trollopian in literary art; he does not concern himself with detail or general statement but he makes some one expressive particular serve for all introduction and explanation of a fact." [3] And in *Criticism and Fiction* he states, "When realism becomes false to itself, when it heaps up facts merely, and maps life instead of picturing it, realism will perish too. . . . Every true realist knows this, and it is perhaps the reason he is so careful of every fact, and feels himself bound to express or indicate its meaning at the risk of over-moralizing." [4]

But in the total body of Howells' *Atlantic* criticism one does not feel the concern about the anti-aesthetic dangers in realism which disturbed both Lathrop and Perry. In other words, though both Howells and Lathrop would have subscribed to Emily Dickinson's view that the writer's task is to distill "attars so immense/From the familiar species," Howells' chief interest in his reviews is likely to be in the discovery in fiction of the familiar species; Lathrop's emphasis is frequently upon the importance of distillation.

For Lathrop is a realist whose views have been strongly modified by the Hawthorne tradition. Thus he believes that "no novelist possessing genuine insight can fail to be in some sort an idealist. His personal impressions and keen, unswerving perceptions must enter into the substance of his creation; idea will insensibly enter into every item of the representation." [5]

As his review of James's *The American* indicates, he finds "a symbolic quality essential to the best artistic success." [6] And Scudder commends Lathrop's own novel *An Echo of Passion* for "its masterly development of the central motif." [7]

Scudder's position may perhaps be most easily clarified by setting certain of his views against the later critical pronouncements of Howells, for we have enough of Scudder's own comments on Howells to illustrate the differences between the two men. In general it may be said that Scudder prefers broad rather than detailed treatment; that he asks for the use of the significant rather than the merely characteristic; that he favors "story" and "ending" rather than "a slice of life"; and that he sometimes admits that he is weary of the very realism for which Howells, especially by the latter half of the 1880's, is actively crusading. In his critical practice he is inclined to devote more attention to aesthetic considerations than does Howells, for in "The Editor's Study" in *Harper's Magazine* Howells' chief interest lies in pleading the case for a democratic realism.

One of Scudder's most vigorous protests against what seems to him to be too minute analysis is in his review of *Criticism and Fiction*. "If our ancestors could read some of the microscopic fiction of the present day," he writes, "we suspect that they would cry out for something more in mass, less in detail." They might agree, he thinks, that "the touch of Nature is there," but they might also protest that they "prefer Nature in larger form, leopards instead of grasshoppers, no matter how truthful the latter may be." [8] This opposition to excessive use of details and to intensive psychological analysis is indicated also by his preference for writers whose work is "large, imaginative, and constantly responsive to the elemental movements of human nature." [9] He writes, "We hope that the coming novelist, if he is heir to the grace and distinct naturalness of Mr. Howells, will have something of the large, vigorous imaginative vividness which are the undeniable properties of Mr. Harte's fiction." [10] And he praises the work of George Washington Cable, Mary Noailles Murfree, Mary Hartwell Catherwood, and Francis Marion Crawford on similar grounds.

Another of his demands is for selection of significant details. Writing of Howells' *A Modern Instance* he suggests that "it is a dull imagination which needs all the details Mr. Howells has given" and advises him to "choose that which is significant not merely that which is characteristic." [11] Though Howells would probably say that "the crossing of the Rubicon was not momentous in itself," Scudder believes that the novelist "lessens the meaning of every selected act by making no one of them especially significant." [12] Moreover, as we have already noted, he believes that it is an artist's duty to bring his work to an aesthetic conclusion.

Scudder's emphasis on "story," his interest in such a writer as Francis Marion Crawford, and his occasional blunt complaint that "realism holds us in chains" [13] all indicate that he is a far less thorough-going realist than Howells. Even when we set against these views Scudder's warnings about wire-drawn stories, his high praise for a book like James's *The Tragic Muse*,[14] and his admiration for several of Howells' own novels, we must still conclude that his realism is always a modified one. Yet the very moderation of his views makes him a more judicial critic than has perhaps yet been recognized.

When Scudder complains that Howells, in *Criticism and Fiction*, is hardly a critic in the usual sense but rather "an apostle, ardently declaring his gospel," he puts his finger on one of the chief differences between his own criticism and that of Howells. As Scudder suggests further, "In his eagerness to preach his doctrines he ignores the offenses of those whom he holds to have the true faith at heart, and overlooks the shining virtues of those who are to him worshippers of false gods." [15] The charge seems a legitimate one, though it can hardly be denied that there are times when a movement may be well served by a propagandist.

At any rate, it is true that during the years that Howells, in "The Editor's Study," is centering attention on realistic values, especially democratic ones, Scudder, though not ignoring realism, is giving more attention than Howells to artistic problems. Thus, whereas Scudder may call attention to Miss Murfree's economy in portraiture or to her excessive use of nature description, Howells may take note of Miss Murfree in order to make an impassioned plea for realism. Howells writes, "The perfect portrayal of what passes even in a soul whose body smokes a cob-pipe or dips snuff, and dwells in a log hut on a mountain side, would be worth all the fancies feigned; and we value Miss Murfree's work for the degree in which it approaches this perfection." [16] Artistic matters may be dismissed by Howells in a sentence or two, as when he writes of Mrs. Ward's *Robert Elsmere* that "the art is almost equal to the strain an obvious purpose puts upon art." [17] Scudder, as we have seen, has a good deal more to say to Mrs. Ward about the necessity of judging works of art by the laws of art. Howells' review of Bellamy's *Looking Backward* quickly classifies the book as a romance, having frank elements of allegory, and then adds, "You concede the premises, as in a poem, and after that you can hold the author only to a poetic consistency." [18] Howells is then free to praise the contents of the book. Scudder, less convinced than Howells by Bellamy's argument, which he thinks has the defect of ignoring human nature, is likewise more dubious about the form of the novel. "In a strict classification," he writes, "we should hesitate to place [it] under the head of fiction." [19]

Howells' progress toward critical realism, revealed by comparing his *Atlantic* reviews with his later critical theories,[20] need not be treated here, for our concern is with the pattern of *Atlantic* criticism itself. But we should speak briefly of certain chronological variations within that *Atlantic* pattern, for recognition of such variations may help to clarify the history of fictional theory during the period.

George Eliot might be said to represent the first stage of *Atlantic* criticism, that of interest in realistic portrayal of scene and character and in plausible motivation. And she continues to stand as a model for a cause and effect development of character. But by the 1870's there is a shift from George Eliot to Turgénieff, a shift that is marked by increased emphasis on the aesthetic aspects of fiction. Not only is there greater emphasis on beauty as well as reality, on the ideal as well as the real, and on imagination as well as on observation; but there is also a tendency to favor chiefly those writers whose work is free from authorial digressions and whose portrayal of character is handled dramatically. Thus Turgénieff stands, during the 1870's, as a convenient standard for evaluating not only the literalism of Trollope and the scientific aims of Zola but also the aesthetic errors of George Eliot.

In the two following decades other changes appear in the critical picture. To be sure, many of the principles which in the 1870's were used in the criticism of Turgénieff and Trollope appear in the 1890's in discussions of Francis Marion Crawford, Henry James, and William Dean Howells. But there are differences within these principles which should be briefly suggested. During the early years of the *Atlantic,* for instance, there is perhaps greater interest in what might be called the philosophic validity of realism, more frequent reference to the imagination in terms of its function of piercing the actual to discover its Platonic reality. Once again we must speak in terms of emphasis, for as late as 1898 Henry D. Sedgwick expresses his dissatisfaction with realism in Platonic terms as he writes, " 'Let us get at facts,' said the crowd; but they could not, for the facts of life are spirit which appear only to the crowd in multitudinous disguises." [21] And certainly Scudder is just as eager to have fiction reveal the universal in the particular as are Perry and Lathrop.

But the focus of the particular might almost be said to have changed. Early realists had been content to give more or less detailed transcriptions of actual scenes, customs, and dialect. Later realists, however, came to depend more often upon an intensive psychological analysis which not only tended to substitute case histories for novels but which also seemed, especially to Scudder, to be untrue to the broad outlines of life. Thus for Scudder the term "imagination" seems at times to mean a breadth of approach which, by not seeing life too minutely, sees it more clearly. The demand for dramatic portrayal of character remains, but the focus of objection is now less against the generalized philosophic digressions of the author than against the novelist's explicit analysis of the intricate psychological processes of his persons.

Literalism might, likewise, be said to have become more self-conscious and, through the comments of Howells and of Garland,[22] to have invaded the field of fictional theory. To Scudder and to Paul Shorey the realists' desire to reproduce life in fiction by merely following the day by day course of an individual's existence could only mean the denial of art. It is in direct answer to Howells that Shorey writes, "What Mr. Howells calls the 'foolish old superstition that literature and art are anything but the expression of life' is really the everlasting truth that literature and art are not merely the satisfaction of the love of imitation, but the exercise and gratification of taste and instincts for symmetry, harmony, unity and definition which life in the ordinary sense fails to satisfy." [23]

Behind these chronological variations, of course, lie corresponding changes in the general cultural pattern of the age, most significant of which is undoubtedly the growing importance of scientific thinking. The relation of science to literature is a problem which deserves attention in a separate study,[24] but we should at least suggest the relation of science and scientific method to the fictional standards which we have noted in this study. As Mr. Robert Mitchell has shown in a recent dissertation, there was considerable interest in the *Atlantic* in scientific matters.[25] And that interest is likewise revealed both directly and indirectly in *Atlantic* criticism.

It is true, of course, that certain of the fictional standards which we have considered can be explained in part in terms of the familiar literary cycle, in this case the reaction against romanticism. Approval given to the use of recognizable locality is, from one point of view, an answer to the use of unreal locales in romantic fiction; attention to life-like characters is a response to the paper heroes and heroines of melodrama; emphasis on action which reveals plausible motivation is a reaction against the thrilling but implausible adventures of the same school. But many of these standards also bear the mark of the century's increasing concern with science.

There is, first of all, the very frequent demand for actual fact. The question raised by Thomas Sergeant Perry of "how much the predominance of novel making at the present time is due to this curiosity for detail . . . " [26] is one which can hardly be answered. But when we consider the part which observation and recording of fact play in *Atlantic* critical standards, we are reminded of the "concern with the external world" which, according to F. O. Matthiessen, "came to mark every phase of the century's increasing closeness of observation, whether in such scientific achievements as the lenses for the telescope and the microscope, or in the painter's new experiments with light, or in the determination of the photographers and the realistic novelists to record every specific surface detail." [27] Certainly the truth of Matthiessen's statement is borne out by much of the *Atlantic* criticism we have discussed, whether it be in the demand that fiction ground its productions on actual truth or in the reminder "to the scurrying band of writers now ranging the globe in search of new literary materials" that "a fresh vision is worth more than a fresh fact." [28] "Of most of our writers it is true to say that they feel a far stronger obligation to write with an eye on the object than they would have felt ten years ago," [29] writes C. T. Copeland in 1892. And his comment may well stand as a partial characterization of much of the fictional practice, and of the fictional theory, during a period when science, in Max Eastman's phrase, was in "a fact-gathering phase." [30]

But though the "absolute, unconditional reverence for facts" [31] is an important part of the history of realism, there are other aspects of the realistic movement which also show reflections of science. The emphasis placed on a cause and effect sequence is perhaps a more important part of the story of realism than we have yet recognized. For such an emphasis has a good deal to do with the reputations of various authors during the period. It is reflected in the popularity of both George Eliot and Ivan Turgénieff. And it is likewise a factor in the diminishing favor accorded such writers as Thackeray, whose stories "too often give the impression of being composed of successive accumulations of incidents and persons, that drift into the story on no principle of artistic selection and combination,"[32] and Dickens, who, in general, "does not develop his characters but conceives them in their entirety at once."[33] Though some of the emphasis on cause and effect in character development may well come from a kind of common sense attitude which recognizes, in Emerson's words, that "Nature has a magic by which she fits the man to his fortunes by making him the fruit of his character,"[34] it seems equally probable that much of the demand results from the growing tendency during the period "to detect in all cases relations of cause and effect."[35] For *Atlantic* criticism speaks too frequently of "the inevitable sequence of cause and effect and its attendant corollaries"[36] for us to escape the conclusion that science, in giving new prestige to the concept of causality, left a very real mark on fiction and on fictional theory. Lida Krockow, in a review of Spielhagen's Memoirs, points out that the psychological habit of determining cause and effect has so modified the form of that author's reminiscences that biographical experiences are treated chiefly as influences.[37] And certainly a similar modification may be observed in the tightening of fictional structure. It is, of course, a cause and effect pattern which is still shaped by a sense of the individual's own responsibility rather than by a deterministic view of heredity and environment. For the fictional hero of the period is a human being whose traits, as revealed in action,[38] determine his pattern of life. The drama is, in other words, that of the individual, not of society as it determines the life of the individual. But in the matter of form the emphasis on causality is leading in the direction of the naturalistic novel.

In fact, one may suggest that if we are to tell fully either the story of realism itself or the history of that movement in relation to science we must give more attention to fictional form than we have yet done.[39] Nor must we forget that *Atlantic* criteria regarding form include also insistence on artistic impartiality, an insistence which bears fruit in the formulation of several new fictional principles. It means the banishment of the intrusive author, it results in open opposition to didacticism, and it is indirectly related to the demand for dramatic presentation.[40] Science can hardly be given full credit for all these standards, for *Atlantic* criticism, offering sharp resistance to Zola's proposal that the novelist take over the methods of the scientist, refuses to equate science and art. But the scientific practice of looking at matters objectively must, nevertheless, be considered as one influence in breaking down what seems to Lathrop an "excess of subjectivity"[41] in many of the novels of the day.

The problem is, of course, a complex one, for pervasive though the influence of science may be suspected to be, affecting even those critics who oppose certain of its encroachments on fiction, there is still a stronge idealistic strain in *Atlantic* standards. Sometimes, in fact, it is strong enough to manifest itself in critical dissatisfaction with realism, as in Scudder's comment, that "we are more disposed to think that what is technically known as realism is a phase of literature which corresponds with much that is contemporary in science and religion but that, far from being the final word in literature, it will simply make its contribution to art and give place to a purer idealism."[42] More often, however, it is present as a background for literary standards, influencing the demand for artistic insight which will give value and definition to the raw material of fiction and which will produce a new artistic reality. What is most noteworthy about the idealistic thinking of the *Atlantic* is the fact that it results in something more than a blind protest

97

against realism. How much of this idealism is directly a product of the Lowell-Hawthorne tradition and how much of it is an expression of intellectual trends within the period itself is, of course, impossible to determine.[43] Whatever its source, however, it does result in a consistent defense of art.

But such speculations on cultural patterns serve chiefly to remind us of the great amount of work to be done on fiction. It does seem evident that it is in the novel, as a relatively undefined form, that we shall find clearer reflections of intellectual and cultural trends than may be observed, for instance, in poetry.[44] And it seems worth noting that these trends should be sought in form as well as in content.

At the moment it is more profitable, perhaps, to turn to a brief assessment of the criticism we have been discussing. There are, of course, certain omissions and blind spots. Those who are interested in seeing a complete reflection of the history of realism, for instance, will at once note the *Atlantic's* failure to recognize those American humorists whose works, as Walter Blair and others have shown,[45] played a considerable part in the rise of realism. Whether a certain gentility or a certain New England sensitiveness is the cause, it is at any rate true that the *Atlantic* did not respond favorably to the Slicks, the Wards, the Nasbys, and the Widow Bedotts. G. S. Hillard writes in December, 1858, that "we confess that . . . we are heartily weary of the Yankee,—we mean as a literary creation,—of the eternal repetition of the character of which Sam Slick is the prototype. . . . "[46] And the following year a review of *High Life in New York* complains, "The sole object seems to be to exhibit the 'Yankee' character in its traditional deformities of stupidity and meanness,—otherwise denominated simplicity and shrewdness."[47] In fact, only Lowell's Hosea Biglow, who is praised at the expense of Ward and Nasby, escapes censure.[48]

Some Conclusions

Nor can Mark Twain be said to attain the prestige in the *Atlantic* that is accorded to many other authors. During Howells' editorship, it is true, there are a number of reviews of his work, and a good deal of praise. And Lathrop speaks of *Life on the Mississippi* as "the most thorough and racy report of the whole phenomena which has yet been forthcoming." [49] But there is little tendency to regard Twain as a force in the development of realism. And Charles Miner Thompson, writing in 1897 that Twain "has recorded the life of certain Southwestern portions of our country, at one fleeting stage of their development, better than it will ever be done again," adds that he "has long been accepted of the people, never of the critics." [50]

The ignoring of Herman Melville[51] might not be worth mention, for neglect of Melville during this period is certainly widespread, were it not for the fact that Howells' review of *Battle Pieces* dismisses that poetry for its lack of realism. That Melville "treats events as realistically as one can to whom they seem to have presented themselves as dreams" [52] is Howells' verdict. One can only speculate whether Howells held similar views of Melville's fiction. One can only speculate, likewise, as to why Stephen Crane's *The Red Badge of Courage* receives no formal review, for the brief annotation in "Comment on New Books" in March, 1896, suggests that "the original power of the book is great enough to set a new fashion in literature." [53]

In light of the standards of taste and morality that we have considered, it is easier to understand why certain other books receive only annotations of two or three sentences. Hardy's *Jude the Obscure,* for instance, is dismissed with the conclusion that its author "sees everything, including the sun in the heavens, through smoked glasses." [54] Of Ambrose Bierce's *Tales of Soldiers and Civilians* a reviewer remarks, "It has never been our fortune to read a collection of tales so uniformly horrible and revolting."[55] George Gissing's *The Odd Women* is merely noted as "an exceptionally interesting and forcible, but, as is the author's wont, a peculiarly dreary and depressing book."[56] Of George Moore's *Esther Waters* it is suggested, "If one wishes to see how a painstaking artist deals with disagreeable material, and keeps his reader's attention to the details of an ill-smelling world, here is the opportunity."[57]

But to dwell on these omissions, important though some recognition of them is, is to obscure the more positive achievements of the *Atlantic*. Offering, for the most part, notices "free from indiscriminate eulogy,"[58] it presents a set of standards which reveal a more consistent policy than one might expect for a period of forty years. It takes seriously the criticism of fiction, placing most of its review volumes in the hands of critics who either have attempted to write fiction themselves or whose experience with literature is a broad one.[59] And it appears more cosmopolitan in its literary interests than has sometimes been thought. For both the attention paid to the local colorists and the wide interest in foreign writers serve to refute the charge of provincialism.[60]

To measure the *Atlantic's* contribution to the fictional development of the period is hardly possible. But it cannot be doubted that, from the beginning of its history, it played a not inconsiderable part in encouraging the rising realism, in bringing the novel closer to "life and manners and motives"[61] through its insistence on believable patterns of experience, based on the pattern of real life.

Credit must also be given for its consistent demand for freedom from authorial interference and for dramatic portrayal of character. Our generation, which knows Henry James better than it perhaps knows the American critical thinking to which he was exposed,[62] has been inclined to give to James the credit for insisting that an author "render," not merely state. Chief credit must continue to go to James, for his is the most distinctive critical statement,[63] as well as the most distinctive practice, of the policy of avoiding a "seated mass of information." Compared with James's subtle revelations of character, *Atlantic* demands for character in action sometimes seem crude; and it can hardly be denied that such demands may now and then find more convenient illustration in the fiction of Francis Marion Crawford than in that of James himself. But it is worth noting that in the attempt to break down essay elements within the novel *Atlantic* criticism is not only solidly behind James but also perhaps makes a positive contribution to fictional theory by applying such standards to the various writers of the period.

Nor should the *Atlantic* defense of art against the threats of science or literalism be discounted. It is the old warfare between science and poetry, fought this time in a period when science was giving to history a new impetus, when the "aesthetic balance between fact and idea"[64] might easily be upset by the stress upon objective reality, and when the desire for accurate transcriptions of life often seemed to make writers neglect art. That art is "a formal creation, not a parcel of information,"[65] that the artist "must organize, not merely duplicate experience"[66] is an *Atlantic* lesson which has had to be repeated by many of our twentieth century critics. But because of its repetition in our own day, we are perhaps better able to evaluate the *Atlantic* position than we were two or three decades ago. Thus modifications of realism in the name of art seem to us something more than mere indications of caution and gentility. Elements of caution, of gentility must be admitted, just as we must admit that it is not Lathrop or Scudder, but Henry James, from whom we have learned many of our fictional principles. But we can, I think, hardly dismiss these critics as "defenders of ideality"[67] or banish them to the limbo of "the academy and the drawing room."[68] For they make a consistent attempt to dignify the novel as a literary form, to make it worthy, as Howells puts it, of the consideration of mature readers.

NOTES

Chapter One

1. 1:256 (December, 1857) Review of Otto Ludwig, *Thüringer Naturen, Charackter und Sittenbilder in Erzählungen.*
2. 1:891-2 (May, 1858) Review of George Eliot, *Scenes of Clerical Life.*
3. *Ibid.*
4. 4:522 (October, 1859) Review of George Eliot, *Adam Bede.*
5. 3:652 (May, 1859) Review of B. F. Presbury, *The Mustee; or Love and Liberty.*
6. 5:621 (May, 1860) E. P. Whipple, "Nathaniel Hawthorne."
7. 5:754 (June, 1860) C. E. Norton, Review of *Mademoiselle Mori; a Tale of Modern Rome.*
8. 6:377 (September, 1860) James Russell Lowell, Review of J. T. Trowbridge, *The Old Battle Ground.* Lowell's review, which is an appreciative one, also commends realistic elements in an earlier novel, Sylvester Judd's *Margaret.*
9. 8:774 (December, 1861) E. P. Whipple, Review of Theodore Winthrop, *Cecil Dreeme.*
10. 9:54 (January, 1862) G. S. Hillard, "James Fenimore Cooper."
11. 10:126-8 (July, 1862) E. P. Whipple, Review of Harriet Beecher Stowe, *The Pearl of Orr's Island.*
12. 9:525-6 (April, 1862) Review of Gustave Merlet, *Le Réalisme et la Fantaisie dans la Littérature.*
13. 10:251 (August, 1862) Review of Henry Kingsley, *Ravenshoe.*
14. 12:154 (August, 1863) C. Nordoff, "Theodore Winthrop's Writings."
15. 14:516 (October, 1864) Thomas Wentworth Higginson, Review of Harriet E. Prescott, *Azarian.*

16. 10:251 (August, 1862) Review of Henry Kingsley, *Ravenshoe*.
17. 17:777 (June, 1866) William Dean Howells, Review of Bayard Taylor, *The Story of Kennett*.
18. 14:666 (December, 1864) "English Authors in Florence."
19. 20:480-81 (October, 1867) H. T. Tuckerman, "The Writings of T. Adolphus Trollope."
20. 21:128 (January, 1868) Review of Bret Harte, *Condensed Novels and Other Papers*.
21. 22:634-5 (November, 1868) W. D. Howells, Review of Edward Everett Hale, *If, Yes, and Perhaps*.
22. 26:506 (October, 1870) W. D. Howells, Review of William Baker, *The New Timothy*. Howells' review of Baker's *Mose Evans* notes "the same intense localization; the thing is southern-southwestern." (34:230, August, 1874).
23. 30:488 (October, 1872) Review of William Flagg, *A Good Investment; a Story of the Upper Ohio*.
24. *Ibid*. Compare Howells' comment on Björnson's *Arne, The Happy Boy, and The Fisher Maiden*: "The facts are stated with perfect ruggedness and downrightness when necessary, but some dreamy haze seems still to cling about them, subduing their harsh outlines and features like the tender light of the slanting Norwegian sun on the craggy Norwegian headlands." (25:508, April, 1870).
25. 29:364 (March, 1872) W. D. Howells, Reviews of Harriet Beecher Stowe, *Oldtown Fireside Stories;* J. W. De Forest, *Kate Beaumont;* and Edward Eggleston, *The Hoosier Schoolmaster*. De Forest's book is here praised as "so life-like that we are persuaded to believe that it is the first full and perfect picture of Southern society of the times before the war." (*Ibid*.) De Forest receives consistent praise for realistic qualities. A review of *Overland* mentions "the vivid descriptions of the strange local life and scenery," the truth of which is said to be verified by those "who are best acquainted with it." (29:111, January, 1872). Clarence Gordon comments of De Forest's sketches, "There is a literalness of surroundings, descriptions of scenery, war records, and political influence that is wonderfully honest." ("Mr. De Forest's Novels," 32:611, November, 1873). Howells says of De Forest that

"so far he is really the only American novelist." (Review of *The Wetherel Affair*, 34:229, August, 1874)
26. 30:487 (October, 1872) Review of William Flagg, *A Good Investment; a Story of the Upper Ohio*.
27. 30:747 (December, 1872) W. D. Howells, Review of Edward Eggleston, *The End of the World*.
28. 46:415 (September, 1880) H. E. Scudder, Review of Frances Hodgson Burnett, *Louisiana*.
29. 25:58-63 (January, 1870) Thomas Wentworth Higginson, "Americanism in Literature."
30. 27:144 (January, 1871) W. D. Howells, Review of Sylvester Judd, *Margaret*. Compare Lowell's characterization of *Miss Gilbert's Career*, by J. G. Holland, as "American from cover to cover." (7:126, January, 1861).
31. 35:737 (June, 1875) W. D. Howells, Review of Constance Fenimore Woolson, *Castle Nowhere; Lake-County Sketches*. The year before, however, Howells had expressed doubt about the possibility of the novel as a form, at least in New England. He notes that Thomas Bailey Aldrich's *Prudence Palfrey* is "told in that semi-idyllic key, into which people writing stories of New England so inevitably fall that we sometimes think that a New England novel is not possible; that our sectional civilization is too narrow, too shy, and too lacking in high and strong contrasts to afford material for the dramatic realism of that kind of fiction. Hawthorne renounced and denounced the idea of such a thing; we all know how Mr. Hale in his bright sketches immaterializes good, honest every-day facts. Dr. Holmes's fictions are rather psychological studies than novels. In fact the New England novel does not exist." (34:228, August, 1874). On the other hand, Howells takes exception to the view expressed in James's *Hawthorne* about the poverty of American backgrounds. He writes with some feeling, "After leaving out all these novelistic 'properties,' as sovereigns, courts, aristocracy, gentry, castles, cottages, cathedrals, abbeys, universities, museums, political class, Epsoms and Ascots, by the absence of which Mr. James suggests our poverty to the English conception, we have the whole of human life remaining, and a social structure pre-

senting the only fresh and novel opportunities left to fiction, opportunities manifold and inexhaustible." (Review of Henry James, *Hawthorne*, 45:284, February, 1880.)
32. 46:831 (December, 1880) H. E. Scudder, Review of George W. Cable, *The Grandissimes*.
33. 46:124 (July, 1880) T. S. Perry, Review of Constance Fenimore Woolson, *Rodman the Keeper*.
34. 34:115 (July, 1874) T. S. Perry, Review of Rebecca Harding Davis, *John Andross*.
35. 41:404 (March, 1878) T. S. Perry, Review of J. L. Crane, *The Two Circuits*.
36. 25:505-12 (April, 1870) W. D. Howells, Review of Björnstjerne Björnson, *Arne, The Happy Boy, The Fisher Maiden*.
37. *Ibid.*
38. 28:126 (July, 1871) Review of Caroline Chesebro, *The Foe in the Household*. Miss Chesebro's work, on the other hand, is found, "very quietly and decently wrought."
39. 45:51 (January, 1880) Harriet W. Preston, Review of B. M. Butt, *Delicia*. Miss Preston writes that Sainte-Beuve himself might have commended *Delicia* for "its delicate truthfulness, its moderation, and simplicity."
40. 25:512 (April, 1870) W. D. Howells, Review of Björnstjerne Björnson, *Arne, The Happy Boy, The Fisher Maiden*.
41. 26:382 (September, 1870) Review of Ruffini, *Carlino*.
42. 34:624 (November, 1874) W. D. Howells, Review of Hjalmar H. Boyesen, *Gunnar*. Howells speaks of "that good school of which Björnson is the head and to which we have nothing answering of English root."
43. 38:450 (October, 1876) T. S. Perry, "George Sand." Perry also praises the simplicity and accuracy of the pictures of Belgian life in *Contes Flamonds et Wallons* by Camille Lemonnier. (35:373, March, 1875).
44. 26:383 (September, 1870) W. D. Howells, Review of Hans Christian Andersen, *O. T.; a Danish Romance*. Though Howells finds "the conception theatrical," he adds that "the reader is everywhere conscious of admirable painting of local and individual life." He calls Andersen's *Only a Fiddler* "full of Denmark as well as humanity," but he complains that the

Notes

author is "a pre-Raphaelite in some things; and he is apt to spend so much time upon the beautiful rendering of particulars in his pictures as to lose his control over the whole effect." (26:632-4, November, 1870).

45. 36:602 (November, 1875) H. E. Scudder, "Andersen's Short Stories." Scudder adds, "Especially is it to be noted that these stories . . . show clearly the coming in of that temper in novel-writing which is eager to describe things as they are."
46. 48:569 (October, 1881) H. E. Scudder, Review of Björnstjerne Björnson, *Synnöve Solbakken*.
47. *Ibid.* Scudder suggests that "stories of unfamiliar races told by one of themselves have peculiar zest and freshness." Perry likewise admits "an added piquancy in stories of foreign life," noting that the local color in many of these stories is "apt to seem more valuable from its novelty than an exact estimate of its merits would warrant." (Review of Henry Gréville, *Dosia; Sonia; Nouvelles Russes*, 42:303, September, 1878)
48. 54:131 (July, 1884) G. P. Lathrop, Review of Charles Egbert Craddock [Mary Noailles Murfree], *In the Tennessee Mountains*.
49. 53:712 (May, 1884) G. P. Lathrop, Review of Sarah Orne Jewett, *The Mate of the Daylight*.
50. 29:363 (March, 1872) W. D. Howells, Review of Edward Eggleston, *The Hoosier Schoolmaster*.
51. 33:111 (January, 1874) Review of Robertson Gray, *Brave Hearts*.
52. 33:745 (June, 1874) W. D. Howells, Review of Edward Eggleston, *The Circuit Rider*.
53. 2:897 (December, 1858) G. S. Hillard, Review of R. T. S. Lowell, *The New Priest in Conception Bay*.
54. 39:759 (June, 1877) W. D. Howells, Review of Sarah Orne Jewett, *Deephaven*. Howells finds that everything is "touched with a hand that holds itself from every trick of exaggeration."
55. 42:194 (August, 1878) H. W. Preston, Review of Julia Fletcher, *Kismet*.
56. 59:266 (February, 1887) H. E. Scudder, Review of Charles Egbert Craddock, *In the Clouds*.

57. 64:123 (July, 1889) H. E. Scudder, Review of Charles Egbert Craddock, *The Despot of Broomsedge Cove.*
58. 59:266 (February, 1887) H. E. Scudder, Review of Charles Egbert Craddock, *In the Clouds.*
59. 54:133 (July, 1884) G. P. Lathrop, Review of Charles Egbert Craddock, *In the Tennessee Mountains.*
60. 56:558 (October, 1885) H. E. Scudder, Review of Charles Egbert Craddock, *The Prophet of the Great Smoky Mountains.*
61. 69:697 (May, 1892) H. E. Scudder, Review of Charles Egbert Craddock, *In the "Stranger People's" Country.*
62. 41:404 (March, 1878) T. S. Perry, Review of J. L. Crane, *The Two Circuits; a Story of Illinois Life.*
63. 39:759 (June, 1877) W. D. Howells, Review of Sarah Orne Jewett, *Deephaven.*
64. 53:713 (May, 1884) G. P. Lathrop, Review of Sarah Orne Jewett, *The Mate of the Daylight.*
65. 67:849 (June, 1891) H. E. Scudder, Reviews of Annie Trumbull Slosson, *Seven Dreamers;* Mary E. Wilkins, *A New England Nun;* Sarah Orne Jewett, *Strangers and Wayfarers.*
66. 73:559 (April, 1894) H. E. Scudder, Review of Kate Chopin, *Bayou Folk.*
67. 75:819 (June, 1895) C. M. Thompson, Review of Rowland Robinson, *Danvis Folks.*
68. 25:762 (June, 1870) Review of Berriedale, *Unforgiven.*
69. 44:383 (September, 1879) W. H. Bishop, "Story-Paper Literature."
70. 34:324 (September, 1874) G. P. Lathrop, "The Novel and its Future."
71. 33:497 (April, 1874) T. S. Perry, Review of Victor Cherbuliez, *Prosper Randoce.*
72. 46:826 (December, 1880) H. E. Scudder, Review of Edward Bellamy, *Dr. Heidenhoff's Process.*
73. 26:251 (August, 1870) Henry James, Review of Benjamin Disraeli, *Lothair.* James finds enough romance in Disraeli's book to make it "pleasant reading for a summer's day" but suggests that it is not a work to be taken with much critical seriousness.

74. 31:359 (March, 1873) Review of Jean Ingelow, *Off the Skelligs.*
75. 51:466 (April, 1883) Charles Dudley Warner, "Modern Fiction."
76. 46:313-4 (September, 1880) T. S. Perry, "Sir Walter Scott."
77. 59:131 (January, 1887) H. E. Scudder, "Stockton's Stories."
78. 57:855 (June, 1886) H. E. Scudder, Review of William Dean Howells, *Indian Summer.*
79. 14:254-6 (August, 1864) Review of Anthony Trollope, *The Small House at Allington.* In his article "The Writings of T. Adolphus Trollope," H. T. Tuckerman reports an interesting conversation with Anthony Trollope. He writes, " 'I am indebted to you for a knowledge of life in the old cathedral towns of England,—of the ecclesiastical side of society, so minute and authentic that it is like a personal experience.' Thus I replied to Anthony Trollope's declaration that he lacked an essential quality of the novelist—imagination. 'Ah,' he replied, 'when you speak of careful observation and honest and thorough report thereof, I am conscious of fidelity to the facts of life and character; but,' he added with that bluff heartiness so characteristic of the man, 'my brother is more than an accurate observer; he is a scholar, a philosopher as well, with historical tastes and cosmopolitan sympathies. . . . You should read his books. . . .'" (20:476, October, 1867).
80. 14:254-6 (August, 1864) Review of Anthony Trollope, *The Small House at Allington.* However, the critic writes, "Mr. Trollope's greatest value, we take it, is that he is so purely a novelist," adding, "The central purpose of a work of fiction is assuredly the portrayal of human passions. To this Mr. Trollope steadfastly adheres."
81. 33:617-8 (May, 1874) T. S. Perry, Review of Anthony Trollope, *Phineas Redux.*
82. 46:835 (December, 1880) H. E. Scudder, Review of Anthony Trollope, *The Duke's Children.*
83. 34:322 (September, 1874) G. P. Lathrop, "The Novel and Its Future."
84. 19:550 (May, 1867) E. P. Whipple, "The Genius of Dickens." The terms "daguerreotype" and "photography" are used fre-

Criticism of Fiction

quently to indicate disapproval. Compare T. S. Perry's comment in his review of Théophile Gautier's *Captain Fracasse* that "in these days when writers of novels so often take photography for their model, it is agreeable to read the work of a man who has a real artistic pleasure in describing the adventures, as well as the surroundings of men and women." (46:125, July, 1880). When Howells defends his "real" grasshopper in *Criticism and Fiction* against the complaints of those who will probably call it photographic, he may have had in mind some of these criticisms.

85. 67:845-6 (June, 1891) H. E. Scudder, "New England in the Short Story" [A group of reviews].
86. 47:118 (January, 1881) T. S. Perry, Review of Émile Zola, *Le Roman Expérimental*.
87. *Ibid*.
88. 45:699 (May, 1880) T. S. Perry, Review of Émile Zola, *Nana*.
89. 45:119 (January, 1880) T. S. Perry, Review of Alphonse Daudet, *Les Rois en Exil*.
90. 45:696 (May, 1880) T. S. Perry, Review of Émile Zola, *Nana*.
91. 47:118 (January, 1881) T. S. Perry, Review of Émile Zola, *Le Roman Expérimental*.
92. 28:248 (August, 1871) Henry James, Review of Gustave Droz, *Around a Spring*. James believes that Droz "has resolved the social forces of his own brief hour into a clearer essence than his great predecessor."
93. 34:321 (September, 1874) G. P. Lathrop, "The Novel and Its Future."
94. 34:242 (August, 1874) T. S. Perry, Review of Gustave Flaubert, *La Tentation de Saint Antoine*.
95. 40:382 (September, 1877) T. S. Perry, Review of Gustave Flaubert, *Trois Contes*.
96. 45:695 (May, 1880) T. S. Perry, Review of Émile Zola, *Nana*.
97. *Ibid*. p. 698.
98. 42:304 (September, 1878) T. S. Perry, Review of Émile Zola, *Une Page d'Amour*.
99. 64:125 (July, 1889) H. E. Scudder, Review of Arthur Sherburne Hardy, *Passe Rose*. Scudder notes that Mr. Hardy's book is "historically effective" without such recourse.

100. 65:124 (January, 1890) H. E. Scudder, Review of William Waldorf Astor, *Sforza; a Story of Milan.*
101. 55:675 (May, 1885) Henry James, "George Eliot's Life."
102. 57:265 (February, 1886) H. E. Scudder, Review of Howard Pyle, *Within the Capes.*
103. 65:125 (January, 1890) H. E. Scudder, Review of Mary Hartwell Catherwood, *The Romance of Dollard.*
104. 72:697 (November, 1893) H. E. Scudder, Review of Mary Hartwell Catherwood, *Old Kaskaskia.*
105. 80:854 (December, 1897) Paul Leicester Ford, Review of S. Weir Mitchell, *Hugh Wynne.*
106. 45:454 (April, 1880) H. W. Preston, "A Woman of Genius" [Madame Henrietta Paalzow].
107. 18:480 (October, 1866) Henry James, "The Novels of George Eliot."
108. 49:848-51 (June, 1882) Henry James, "Alphonse Daudet."
109. 36:760 (December, 1875) T. S. Perry, Review of Gustave Droz, *Les Étangs.*
110. 34:321 (September, 1874) G. P. Lathrop, "The Novel and Its Future."
111. 28:249 (August, 1871) Henry James, Review of Gustave Droz, *Around a Spring.*
112. 49:850 (June, 1882) Henry James, "Alphonse Daudet."
113. 34:317-21 (September, 1874) G. P. Lathrop, "The Novel and its Future."
114. 67:850 (June, 1891) H. E. Scudder, "New England in the Short Story."
115. 34:317-21 (September, 1874) G. P. Lathrop, "The Novel and its Future."
116. *Ibid.*
117. 63:276-80 (February, 1889) H. E. Scudder, Reviews of Joseph Kirkland, *The McVeys;* Edward Eggleston, *The Graysons.*
118. 33:569 (May, 1874) T. S. Perry, "Ivan Turgénieff."
119. 27:265 (February, 1871) T. S. Perry, Review of Alexis Pisemski, *Tausend Seelen.*
120. 31:112 (January, 1873) T. S. Perry, Review of Ivan Turgénieff, *Der Oberst, Der Fatalist, The Lear of the Steppe.*

121. 31:239 (February, 1873) W. D. Howells, Review of Ivan Turgénieff, *Liza*.
122. 32:240 (August, 1873) G. P. Lathrop, Review of Ivan Turgénieff, *On the Eve*.
123. 53:52-3 (January, 1884) Henry James, "Ivan Turgénieff."
124. 44:765 (December, 1879) Clara Barnes Martin, "The Greatest Novelist's Work for Freedom."
125. 33:565 (May, 1874) T. S. Perry, "Ivan Turgénieff."
126. 34:322 (September, 1874) G. P. Lathrop, "The Novel and Its Future."
127. 30:631 (November, 1872) T. S. Perry, Review of Ivan Turgénieff, *Frülingsfluthen*.
128. 30:243 (August, 1872) W. D. Howells, Review of Ivan Turgénieff, *Smoke*.
129. 53:52 (January, 1884) Henry James, "Ivan Turgénieff."
130. 60:206 (August, 1887) Harriet W. Preston, "The Spell of the Russian Writers."
131. 51:464, 468 (April, 1883) Charles Dudley Warner, "Modern Fiction."
132. 67:847 (June, 1891) H. E. Scudder, Review of Mary E. Wilkins, *A New England Nun*.
133. 69:695 (May, 1892) H. E. Scudder, Review of Charles Egbert Craddock, *In the "Stranger People's" Country*.
134. 79:106 (January, 1897) Edith Baker Brown, "James Lane Allen."
135. 71:838 (June, 1893) C. T. Copeland, "Miss Austen and Miss Ferrier."
136. 77:265 (February, 1896) H. E. Scudder, Review of Owen Wister, *Red Man and White*.
137. 78:841 (December, 1896) H. E. Scudder, Review of Mrs. Humphry Ward, *Sir George Tressady*.
138. *Ibid.*, p. 843.
139. 81:143 (January, 1898) Henry D. Sedgwick, Jr., Review of Hall Caine, *The Christian*.
140. 37:621 (May, 1876) W. D. Howells, Review of Mark Twain, *The Adventures of Tom Sawyer*.
141. 29:630 (May, 1872) Review of Jonas Lie, *Den Fremsynte, eller Billeder fra Nordland*.

Notes

142. 26:760 (December, 1870) W. D. Howells, Review of Ralph Keeler, *Vagabond Adventures*.
143. 78:164 (August, 1896) Paul Shorey, "Present Conditions of Literary Production." Shorey feels, however, that we "cannot permanently maintain our present zest of curious interest in the literary reflection of unessential fact." He suggests that the society of Balzac is already "obsolete" and that of Zola is "obsolescent." And he adds, "By the time our rising school of local novelists have recorded every American dialect and taken the precise altitude of *ennui* in their respective towns or Kansas farms, the conditions will have changed so that the whole work will have to be done over...." (*Ibid.,* p. 165.)
144. 58:57 (July, 1886) H. W. Preston, "Ouida."
145. 78:165 (August, 1896) Paul Shorey, "Present Conditions of Literary Production."
146. 33:108 (January, 1874) Christopher Cranch, Review of Thomas Wentworth Higginson, *Oldport Days*.

Chapter Two

1. Joseph Warren Beach, *The Method of Henry James,* Yale University Press, 1918, p. 98.
2. 6:138-40 (August, 1860) W. L. Symonds, "The Carnival of the Romantic."
3. 32:371 (September, 1873) G. P. Lathrop, Review of Miss Thackeray [Mrs. Richmond Ritchie], *Old Kensington*.
4. 41:493 (April, 1878) H. W. Preston, "The Story of Avis, and Other Novels."
5. 68:569 (October, 1891) H. E. Scudder, Review of William Dean Howells, *Criticism and Fiction*. Howells had written that without truth "all graces of style and feats of invention and cunning of construction are so many superfluities of naughtiness." (William Dean Howells, *Criticism and Fiction,* New York: Harper, 1891, p. 100).
6. 1:123 (November, 1857) Review of Charles Reade, *White Lies*.

Criticism of Fiction

7. 4:394 (September, 1859) F. H. Underwood, "The Novels of James Fenimore Cooper."
8. 2:896 (December, 1858) G. S. Hillard, Review of R. T. S. Lowell, *The New Priest in Conception Bay.*" Hillard finds that the events "stand in the relation of accidental and not of necessary construction and might be transposed without doing any harm."
9. 6:119 (July, 1860) E. P. Whipple, Review of Maria Cummins, *El Furedis*. Whipple here protests against the characterization of Mrs. Cummins' earlier work, *The Lamplighter*, as a 'sensation book,' pointing out that "the first hundred and fifty pages were as simple, and as true to ordinary nature, as the daisies and buttercups of the common fields."
10. 9:56 (January, 1862) G. S. Hillard, "James Fenimore Cooper."
11. 14:142 (August, 1864) Harriet E. Prescott, "Charles Reade." Miss Prescott pays tribute, however, to Reade's "reckless, rollicking wit" and his "exuberant vitality."
12. 2:896 (December, 1858) G. S. Hillard, Review of R. T. S. Lowell, *The New Priest in Conception Bay.*
13. 1:891 (May, 1858) Review of George Eliot, *Scenes of Clerical Life.*
14. 45:282 (February, 1880) W. D. Howells, Review of Henry James, *Hawthorne.*
15. Nathaniel Hawthorne, "Preface" to *The House of the Seven Gables* (Boston, 1924), p. 13.
16. 34:231 (August, 1874) Review of Ivan Turgénieff, *Spring Floods.*
17. 5:509 (April, 1860) James Russell Lowell, Review of Nathaniel Hawthorne, *The Marble Faun.*
18. 5:622 (May, 1860) E. P. Whipple, "Nathaniel Hawthorne."
19. *Ibid.*
20. 5:509 (April, 1860) James Russell Lowell, Review of Nathaniel Hawthorne, *The Marble Faun.*
21. 45:282 (February, 1880) W. D. Howells, Review of Henry James, *Hawthorne.*
22. 5:254 (February, 1860) James Russell Lowell, Review of Harriet E. Prescott, *Sir Rohan's Ghost.* Lowell notes that Miss

Prescott "calls her story a Romance, thus absolving it from any cumbersome allegiance to fact. . . ."
23. 31:105 (January, 1873) W. D. Howells, Review of Victor Cherbuliez, *Joseph Noirel's Revenge*.
24. 35:737 (June, 1875) W. D. Howells, Review of Constance Fenimore Woolson, *Castle Nowhere*. Horace Scudder likewise sets different standards for judging the two forms. Of Arthur Sherburne Hardy's *Winds of Destiny*, Scudder writes, "The value of any romance undoubtedly depends upon the psychological truth which is at its base." (58:132, July, 1886).
25. 41:490 (April, 1878) H. W. Preston, Review of William Black, *Green Pastures and Piccadilly*.
26. 20:121 (July, 1867) W. D. Howells, Review of J. W. De Forest, *Miss Ravenel's Conversion from Secession to Loyalty*.
27. *Ibid.*
28. 1:891-2 (May, 1858) Review of George Eliot, *Scenes of Clerical Life*.
29. 18:381-2 (September, 1866) Review of Wilkie Collins, *Armadale*. Although Collins, Reade, and Dickens might all be called accurate observers, their use of surprise and coincidence was not always looked upon favorably by *Atlantic* critics. In an essay "The Genius of Dickens," E. P. Whipple writes of that author, "Observation affords him materials, but he always modifies these materials and works them up into the most fantastic shapes." (19:548, May, 1867).
30. 4:522 (October, 1859) Review of George Eliot, *Adam Bede*.
31. 5:756 (June, 1860) Review of George Eliot, *The Mill on the Floss*.
32. 18:769 (December, 1866) W. D. Howells, Review of Charles Reade, *Griffith Gaunt*.
33. 30:495 (October, 1872) T. S. Perry, Review of Gustave Droz, *Babolain*.
34. 30:631 (November, 1872) T. S. Perry, Review of Ivan Turgénieff, *Spring Floods*. Perry calls the hero of Turgénieff's *Helena* "a compound as rare in novels as it is frequent in life, of good and bad qualities." (29:114, January, 1872).
35. 18:481 (October, 1866) Henry James, "The Novels of George Eliot."

36. 42:703 (December, 1878) H. W. Preston, Review of *Colonel Dunwoddie, Millionaire.*
37. 46:123 (July, 1880) T. S. Perry, Review of *Mademoiselle de Mersac.*
38. 31:491 (April, 1873) A. G. Sedgwick, Review of George Eliot, *Middlemarch.*
39. *Ibid.*
40. 43:500-2 (April, 1879) H. W. Preston, Review of Thomas Hardy, *The Return of the Native.*
41. 25:247 (February, 1870) W. D. Howells, Review of William Makepeace Thackeray, *Miscellanies; Catherine.*
42. 25:633-4 (May, 1870) W. D. Howells, Review of Bret Harte, *The Luck of Roaring Camp and Other Stories.*
43. 41:406 (March, 1878) T. S. Perry, Review of Ausburn Towner, *Chedayne of Kotono.*
44. 45:44-5 (January, 1880) H. W. Preston, Review of George Washington Cable, *Old Creole Days.*
45. 40:111 (July, 1877) T. S. Perry, Review of William Black, *Madcap Violet.* Black's book does not meet Perry's standard. He writes that "one revolts at having such dire events spring from so trivial a cause."
46. 54:805 (December, 1884) G. P. Lathrop, "Combination Novels."
47. 78:164 (August, 1896) Paul Shorey, "Present Conditions of Literary Production."
48. 69:126 (January, 1892) Sophia Kirk, Review of Paul Bourget, *Nouveaux Pastels.* Miss Kirk writes, "The French are masters of literary art, and they are often tempted by this supremacy to sacrifice to an artistic unity, which is apt to be an artificial one, the real unity of development, sequence, and accident in human life."
49. 1:639 (March, 1858) James Russell Lowell, Review of F. D. Guerrazzi, *Beatrice Cenci.*
50. 4:130 (July, 1859) Review of Charles Reade, *Love Me Little, Love Me Long.*
51. 4:744 (December, 1859) Review of *Sword and Gown.*
52. 39:632 (May, 1877) H. W. Preston, Review of Philip Gilbert Hamerton, *Wenderholme.*

53. 20:120 (July, 1867) W. D. Howells, Review of J. W. De Forest, *Miss Ravenel's Conversion from Secession to Loyalty.*
54. 34:229 (August, 1874) W. D. Howells, Review of Thomas Bailey Aldrich, *Prudence Palfrey.*
55. 32:371 (September, 1873) G. P. Lathrop, Review of Miss Thackeray [Mrs. Richmond Ritchie], *Old Kensington.*
56. 33:686 (June, 1874) G. P. Lathrop, "Growth of the Novel."
57. 11:239 (February, 1863) A. M. Waterston, "Jane Austen."
58. 33:691 (June, 1874) G. P. Lathrop, "Growth of the Novel."
59. 1:891-2 (May, 1858) Review of George Eliot, *Scenes of Clerical Life.*
60. 35:507 (April, 1875) T. S. Perry, Review of Julian Schmidt, *Bilder aus dem geistigen Leben unserer Zeit.* Commenting on Schmidt's discussion of *Middlemarch,* Perry remarks that "both the English and American public are too much weighted down by George Eliot's greatness to be able to define her position with exactness."
61. 5:756-7 (June, 1860) Review of George Eliot, *The Mill on the Floss.*
62. 18:488 (October, 1866) Henry James, "The Novels of George Eliot." Constantius, one of the characters in James's *"Daniel Deronda;* a Conversation," remarks, "I think there is little art in *Deronda,* but I think there is a vast amount of life." (38:694, December, 1876).
63. 37:285 (March, 1876) T. S. Perry, "Victor Cherbuliez." Unlike George Eliot, Cherbuliez "observes and records without comment."
64. 40:383 (September, 1877) T. S. Perry, Review of Friedrich Spielhagen, *Sturmflut.* Perry remarks that Spielhagen's book "has the clumsy form which George Eliot's genius has taught us to tolerate."
65. 46:697 (November, 1880) W. D. Howells, "Mr. Aldrich's Fiction." Howells adds, "We are not sure that a novelist does not weaken his work by every good thing that he says in his own person."
66. 45:685-6 (May, 1880) H. E. Scudder, Review of Sarah Orne Jewett, *Old Friends and New.*

67. 54:133 (July, 1884) G. P. Lathrop, Review of Charles Egbert Craddock, *In the Tennessee Mountains.*
68. 72:694 (November, 1893) H. E. Scudder, Review of Francis Marion Crawford, *Pietro Ghisleri.*
69. 45:685-6 (May, 1880) H. E. Scudder, Review of Sarah Orne Jewett, *Old Friends and New.*
70. 35:494 (April, 1875) W. D. Howells, Review of Henry James, *A Passionate Pilgrim and Other Tales.* Howells feels, however, that "it would be better if the assumed narrator were to keep himself from seeming to patronize the simple-hearted heroes, and from openly rising above them in a worldly way."
71. 33:689 (June, 1874) G. P. Lathrop, "Growth of the Novel."
72. 32:371 (September, 1873) G. P. Lathrop, Review of Miss Thackeray [Mrs. Richmond Ritchie], *Old Kensington.* Lathrop continues, "To the artist, however, who must ever feel to the quick how much good there is in the bad, how much bad in the good, human individualities are but forces to be poised one with another, in noble and harmonious design."
73. 51:467 (April, 1883) C. D. Warner, "Modern Fiction."
74. 32:614 (November, 1873) Clarence Gordon, "Mr. De Forest's Novels."
75. 65:568 (April, 1890) H. E. Scudder, Review of Charles Dudley Warner, *A Little Journey in the World.*
76. 46:413 (September, 1880) H. E. Scudder, Review of Mrs. A. D. Whitney, *Odd or Even.*
77. 52:123 (July, 1883) H. E. Scudder, Review of Frances Hodgson Burnett, *Through One Administration.*
78. 49:127 (January, 1882) H. E. Scudder, Review of Henry James, *The Portrait of a Lady.*
79. 43:168 (February, 1879) H. W. Preston, Review of Henry James, *The Europeans.*
80. 46:126 (July, 1880) T. S. Perry, Review of Henry James, *Confidence.*
81. 49:129 (January, 1882) H. E. Scudder, Review of William Dean Howells, *Dr. Breen's Practice.*
82. 57:259 (February, 1886) H. E. Scudder, Review of Arlo Bates, *A Wheel of Fire.* Scudder writes that here "the men and

Notes

women are real, without relying upon an indefinite number of minute touches."
83. 65:128 (January, 1890) H. E. Scudder, Review of Constance Fenimore Woolson, *Jupiter Lights.*
84. 78:272-3 (August, 1896) Review of Frances Hodgson Burnett, *A Lady of Quality.*
85. 74:271 (August, 1894) G. R. Carpenter, "A Dumas of the Hour" [Stanley J. Weyman].
86. 75:268-9 (February, 1895) W. P. Trent, Review of Hall Caine, *The Manxman.*
87. 80:510 (October, 1897) Henry D. Sedgwick, "Gabrielle D'Annunzio." Sedgwick fears "lest the portrayal of psychic states constitute the novel, and lest the plots and the poor little incidents squeeze in with much discomfort."
88. 51:468 (April, 1883) C. D. Warner, "Modern Fiction."
89. 33:686 (June, 1874) G. P. Lathrop, "Growth of the Novel." Lathrop is quoting from Fielding's *Amelia.*
90. 75:658 (May, 1895) H. E. Scudder, "New Figures in Literature and Art: Richard Harding Davis."
91. 33:689 (June, 1874) G. P. Lathrop, "Growth of the Novel."
92. *Ibid.*
93. 5:754 (June, 1860) C. E. Norton, Review of *Mademoiselle Mori.*
94. 17:777 (June, 1866) W. D. Howells, Review of Bayard Taylor, *The Story of Kennett.*
95. 23:762 (June, 1869) W. D. Howells, Review of Berthold Auerbach, *Edelweiss.*
96. 29:363 (March, 1872) W. D. Howells, Review of Edward Eggleston, *The Hoosier Schoolmaster.*
97. 37:621 (May, 1876) W. D. Howells, Review of Mark Twain, *The Adventures of Tom Sawyer.*
98. 34:624 (November, 1874) W. D. Howells, Review of Hjalmar Hjorth Boyesen, *Gunnar.*
99. 38:244 (August, 1876) G. P. Lathrop, Review of Thomas Hardy, *The Hand of Ethelberta.*
100. 40:631 (November, 1877) G. P. Lathrop, Review of Frances Hodgson Burnett, *That Lass o' Lowrie's.*

101. 45:51 (January, 1880) H. W. Preston, Review of B. M. Butt, *Delicia*.
102. 33:693 (June, 1874) G. P. Lathrop, "Growth of the Novel."
103. 32:240 (August, 1873) G. P. Lathrop, Review of Ivan Turgénieff, *On the Eve*. In a review of Turgénieff's *Liza,* Howells calls Turgénieff "the most self-forgetful of the story-telling tribe." (31:239, February, 1873).
104. 32:369-70 (September, 1873) W. D. Howells, Review of Ivan Turgénieff, *Dmitri Roudine*. "For all the looseness of construction," Howells writes, "it is a very great novel, as much greater than the novel of incident as Hamlet is greater than Richard III." And though he suggests, "We are not quite sure whether we like or dislike the carefulness with which Roudine's whole character is kept from us, so that we pass from admiration to despite before we come to half-respectful compassion," he adds, "and yet is this not the way it would be in life?"
105. 33:569 (May, 1874) T. S. Perry, "Ivan Turgénieff."
106. *Ibid.*
107. 53:52 (January, 1884) Henry James, "Ivan Turgénieff."
108. 75:817 (June, 1895) C. M. Thompson, Review of Rowland Robinson, *Danvis Folks*.
109. 61:844 (June, 1888) H. E. Scudder, Review of Ellen Olney Kirk, *Queen Money*.
110. 64:122 (July, 1889) H. E. Scudder, Review of Charles Egbert Craddock, *The Despot of Broomsedge Cove*.
111. 54:803-4 (December, 1884) G. P. Lathrop, "Combination Novels."
112. 50:111 (July, 1882) H. E. Scudder, Review of Constance Fenimore Woolson, *Anne*.
113. 42:299 (September, 1878) T. S. Perry, Review of Alphonse Daudet, *Le Nabab*.
114. 40:636 (November, 1877) T. S. Perry, Review of Wilhelm Jensen, *Fluth und Ebbe*.
115. 57:271 (February, 1886) H. E. Scudder, Review of William Waldorf Astor, *Valentino*.
116. 55:127 (January, 1885) H. E. Scudder, Review of E. W. Howe, *The Story of a Country Town*.

Notes

117. 55:847 (June, 1885) H. E. Scudder, Review of Henry F. Keenan, *Trajan*.
118. 73:556 (April, 1894) H. E. Scudder, Review of Henry B. Fuller, *The Cliff Dwellers*.
119. 69:700 (May, 1892) C. T. Copeland, Review of Thomas Hardy, *Tess of the D'Urbervilles*.
120. 65:125 (January, 1890) H. E. Scudder, Review of Mary Hartwell Catherwood, *The Romance of Dollard*.
121. 69:696 (May, 1892) H. E. Scudder, Review of Charles Egbert Craddock, *In the "Stranger People's" Country*. Miss Murfree meets several other requirements of the *Atlantic*. She "has completed her analysis of characters before she draws them" and "as a rule, all is translated unto the terms of speech and behavior and given so clear a tone, so sharp an accent that the meaning cannot be mistaken." (*Ibid.*, p. 695).
122. 59:130 (January, 1887) H. E. Scudder, "Stockton's Stories."
123. 73:133 (January, 1894) H. E. Scudder, "Miss Jewett."
124. 51:469 (April, 1883) C. D. Warner, "Modern Fiction."
125. *Ibid.*
126. 40:508 (October, 1877) H. E. Scudder, Review of *Nimport*.
127. 68:569 (October, 1891) H. E. Scudder, Review of William Dean Howells, *Criticism and Fiction*.
128. 59:130 (January, 1887) H. E. Scudder, "Stockton's Stories."
129. 54:803-4 (December, 1884) G. P. Lathrop, "Combination Novels."
130. 57:853 (June, 1886) H. E. Scudder, Review of Francis Marion Crawford, *A Tale of a Lonely Parish*.
131. 65:123 (January, 1890) H. E. Scudder, Review of Francis Marion Crawford, *Sant' Ilario*. Scudder warns, however, against "the machinery of fiction." Compare his comment on Brander Matthews' *Last Meeting* that "it would be a relief to many readers if they could again get stories in place of attenuated novels; but then they do not want wire-drawn stories." (57:263, February, 1886).
132. 51:410-11 (March, 1883) G. P. Lathrop, Review of Francis Marion Crawford, *Mr. Isaacs*.
133. *Ibid.*, pp. 409-10.

Criticism of Fiction

134. 72:694 (November, 1893) H. E. Scudder, Review of Francis Marion Crawford, *Pietro Ghisleri*.
135. 53:278 (February, 1884) H. E. Scudder, Review of Francis Marion Crawford, *To Leeward*.
136. 60:414 (September, 1887) H. E. Scudder, Review of Francis Marion Crawford, *Saracinesca*.
137. 34:316 (September, 1874) G. P. Lathrop, "The Novel and its Future." Lathrop uses the phrase of Wilkie Collins.
138. 80:857 (December, 1897) C. M. Thompson, Review of Mary E. Wilkins, *Jerome*.
139. 80:143 (July, 1897) H. E. Scudder, Review of James Lane Allen, *The Choir Invisible*.

Chapter Three

1. 5:509 (April, 1860) James Russell Lowell, Review of Nathaniel Hawthorne, *The Marble Faun*.
2. 33:575 (May, 1874) T. S. Perry, "Ivan Turgénieff." Like his colleagues, Perry insists that moral teaching in fiction be indirect. In his essay "Victor Cherbuliez" he writes, "Every man who writes a novel . . . teaches, more or less, even if against his will, by adding some new thing to our experience and contributing in some measure to the moulding of our character." (37:286, March, 1876).
3. 32:369-70 (September, 1873) W. D. Howells, Review of Ivan Turgénieff, *Dmitri Roudine*.
4. 33:695 (June, 1874) G. P. Lathrop, "Growth of the Novel." Lathrop feels that the manner of treatment is important in securing moral insight. He writes of Dickens, whom he considers "antic" in his presentations, that he "succeeds in exciting the reader's instinctive repugnance for uncovered vice . . . but he could never arouse in this way a deep, clear and purifying moral perception." (*Ibid.*, p. 691).
5. 65:731 (June, 1890) C. D. Warner, "The Novel and the Common School."
6. 37:113 (January, 1876) H. E. Scudder, Review of E. C. Stedman, *Victorian Poets*.

Notes

7. 31:239 (February, 1873) W. D. Howells, Review of Ivan Turgénieff, *Liza*.
8. 30:243 (August, 1872) W. D. Howells, Review of Ivan Turgénieff, *Smoke*.
9. 60:201 (August, 1887) H. W. Preston, "The Spell of the Russian Writers."
10. 34:231 (August, 1874) Review of Ivan Turgénieff, *Spring Floods*.
11. 31:490 (April, 1873) A. G. Sedgewick, Review of George Eliot, *Middlemarch*.
12. 5:756 (June, 1860) Review of George Eliot, *The Mill on the Floss*.
13. 42:196-7 (August, 1878) H. W. Preston, Review of Hesba Stretton, *Through a Needle's Eye*.
14. 33:694 (June, 1874) G. P. Lathrop, "Growth of the Novel."
15. *Ibid.*, pp. 695-6.
16. 18:768 (December, 1866) W. D. Howells, Review of Charles Reade, *Griffith Gaunt; or, Jealousy*. Howells compares Reade's book with *Romola* to illustrate "the difference that passes between an artificial and an artistic solution of a moral problem."
17. 28:249-51 (August, 1871) Henry James, Review of Gustave Droz, *Around a Spring*.
18. 28:384 (September, 1871) W. D. Howells, Review of Charles Reade, *A Terrible Temptation*.
19. 33:695 (June, 1874) G. P. Lathrop, "Growth of the Novel."
20. *Ibid.*
21. 15:379 (March, 1865) T. W. Higginson, Review of Jean Ingelow, *Studies for Stories*.
22. 29:110 (January, 1872) Review of Mrs. A. D. Whitney, *Real Folks*.
23. 42:300 (September, 1878) T. S. Perry, Review of Honoré de Balzac, *Les Petits Bourgeois*.
24. 34:435 (October, 1874) Thomas Sergeant Perry, "Berthold Auerbach."
25. 34:363 (September, 1874) W. D. Howells, Review of F. H. Underwood, *Lord of Himself*.

26. 21:761 (June, 1868) W. D. Howells, Review of Henry Ward Beecher, *Norwood*.
27. 55:121-2 (January, 1885) H. E. Scudder, Review of George Washington Cable, *Dr. Sevier*. A few years later in a review of Cable's *Bonaventure* Scudder again notes that the world of Cable's art is "governed by some doctrinaire spectre" and advises, "Let his fine purposes be wholly dramatized and no longer possess him, when he is writing books." (61:842, June, 1888).
28. 55:673 (May, 1885) Henry James, "George Eliot's Life."
29. 38:694 (December, 1876) Henry James, *"Daniel Deronda; a Conversation."*
30. 46:123 (July, 1880) T. S. Perry, Review of *Mademoiselle de Mersac*.
31. 64:531 (October, 1889) Agnes Repplier, "Fiction in the Pulpit."
32. 55:123 (January, 1885) H. E. Scudder, Review of S. Weir Mitchell, *In War Time*.
33. 45:118-19 (January, 1880) T. S. Perry, Review of Alphonse Daudet, *Les Rois en Exil*.
34. 28:383 (September, 1871) W. D. Howells, Review of Charles Reade, *A Terrible Temptation*.
35. 26:128 (July, 1870) Review of Mrs. C. A. Steele, *So Runs the World Away*.
36. 32:653 (December, 1873) L. J. Jennings, "Disraeli."
37. 36:111 (July, 1875) T. S. Perry, Review of Frank Lee Benedict, *Mr. Vaughan's Heir*. Although *Atlantic* criticism ignores many of the sentimental and sensational writers of the day, it frequently censures unhealthiness of tone among those works which it does review. The critic of Berriedale's *Unforgiven*, for instance, prefers that ladies should not write on such subjects as this author has chosen. (25:762, June 1870) And a review of Hawley Smart's *A Race for a Wife* expresses relief that some women writers are "merely vapid, silly, and inconsequent, as Hawley Smart is." (26:256, August, 1870).
38. 28:383-4 (September, 1871) W. D. Howells, Review of Charles Reade, *A Terrible Temptation*. Howells questions, "Is it something in Mr. Reade's tone or manner? . . . Is it a

certain rudeness in handling facts from which there is, by the consent of civilization, a general shrinking?"
39. 27:144 (January, 1871) W. D. Howells, Review of Sylvester Judd, *Margaret*.
40. 32:615 (November, 1873) Clarence Gordon, "Mr. De Forest's Novels."
41. 51:471 (April, 1883) C. D. Warner, "Modern Fiction."
42. 50:267-8 (August, 1882) H. E. Scudder, Review of Bret Harte, *Sketches and Stories*. Howells, writing of Miss Woolson's *Castle Nowhere,* remarks that the work has "a high truth to human nature never once weakened by any vagueness of the moral ideal in the author, as happens with Mr. Harte's sketches." (35:737, June, 1875).
43. 55:127 (January, 1885) H. E. Scudder, Review of E. W. Howe, *The Story of a Country Town.*
44. 79:108 (January, 1897) Edith Baker Brown, "James Lane Allen."
45. 32:240 (August, 1873) G. P. Lathrop, Review of Ivan Turgénieff, *On the Eve.*
46. 38:479 (October, 1876) E. P. Whipple, *"Oliver Twist."*
47. 53:278-9 (February, 1884) H. E. Scudder, Review of Francis Marion Crawford, *To Leeward.*
48. 69:697 (May, 1892) C. T. Copeland, Review of Thomas Hardy, *Tess of the D'Urbervilles*. Several critics express doubt about Hardy. G. P. Lathrop, in a review of *The Hand of Ethelberta,* suggests that Hardy is "perhaps a better artist than either George Eliot or William Black" but finds him limited by his "want of moral inspiration." (38:244, August, 1876). In reviewing *The Trumpet Major,* Scudder complains that "it really seems as if in the world of Mr. Hardy's fiction truth was a plaything to be tossed about in sport." (47:712, May, 1881).
49. 57:260 (February, 1886) H. E. Scudder, Review of Arlo Bates, *A Wheel of Fire.*
50. 77:701 (May, 1896) Lida Krockow, "Hermann Sudermann."
51. 38:449 (October, 1876) T. S. Perry, "George Sand." Perry writes of George Sand herself, "If these novels contained nothing but vicious sentiment and false reasoning, they might

well be left to the natural disdain the reader would feel for them; but in fact what is poisonous is hidden beneath good drawing of character and impassioned eloquence, so that the reader is led to sympathize with all sorts of uncommendable things of which he cannot really approve." (*Ibid.*, p. 447). Few French writers escape some censure. E. P. Whipple thinks it likely that Victor Hugo's *Les Misérables* will "wield a more pernicious influence than Byron ever exerted." (10:125, July, 1862). And Eugene Benson's essay on Théophile Gautier notes the "questionable taste" of that author. (21:668, June, 1868).

52. 38:449 (October, 1876) T. S. Perry, "George Sand."
53. 39:762 (June, 1877) T. S. Perry, Review of Émile Zola, *L'Assommoir*. Perry is not completely accurate in identifying the aesthetic revolt with Zola. For an essay on this subject see Clarence Decker, "The Aesthetic Revolt against Naturalism," *Publications of the Modern Language Association*, LIII (1938), 844-856.
54. 47:575 (April, 1881) T. S. Perry, Review of Gustave Freytag, *Aus einer kleinen Stadt*. Freytag's book offers relief after the unpleasantness of French fiction.
55. 62:712 (November, 1888) Sophia Kirk, Review of Alphonse Daudet, *L'Immortel*.
56. 39:761 (June, 1877) T. S. Perry, Review of Émile Zola, *L'Assommoir*.
57. 45:696 (May, 1880) T. S. Perry, Review of Émile Zola, *Nana*.
58. *Ibid.*, p. 699.
59. 47:116-17 (January, 1881) T. S. Perry, Review of Émile Zola, *Le Roman Expérimental*.
60. *Ibid.*
61. 13:133 (January, 1864) M. A. Dodge, Review of Bayard Taylor, *Hannah Thurston*.
62. 29:364 (March, 1872) W. D. Howells, Review of J. W. De Forest, *Kate Beaumont*.
63. 42:298 (September, 1878) T. S. Perry, Review of Alexander Gontcharoff, *Oblomoff*. Howells, in his review of Turgénieff's *Smoke*, writes that the characters are "related to the most

modern aspects of political and social life in Russia." (30:244, August, 1872).
64. 40:124 (July, 1877) T. S. Perry, Review of Ivan Turgénieff, *Terres Vièrges.*
65. 7:125 (January, 1861) James Russell Lowell, Review of J. G. Holland, *Miss Gilbert's Career.*
66. 26:637 (November, 1870) Ralph Keeler, Review of Friedrich Spielhagen, *Hammer and Anvil.*
67. 45:679 (May, 1880) H. E. Scudder, Review of Amanda M. Douglas, *Hope Mills; or, Between Friend and Sweetheart.*
68. 45:47 (January, 1880) H. W. Preston, Review of Jean Ingelow, *Sarah de Berenger.* Miss Preston adds, "Just so the question of pauper immigration was dragged into *Off the Skelligs.*"
69. 48:566 (October, 1881) Review of *Baby Rue.*
70. 46:418 (September, 1880) H. E. Scudder, Review of Helen Campbell, *Unto the Third and Fourth Generations.*
71. 38:250 (August, 1876) T. S. Perry, Review of Alphonse Daudet, *Jack.*
72. 37:239 (February, 1876) G. P. Lathrop, Review of J. W. De Forest, *Playing the Mischief.*
73. 47:119 (January, 1881) H. E. Scudder, Review of Albion Tourgée, *Bricks Without Straw.*
74. *Ibid.*
75. 75:824 (June, 1895) H. E. Scudder, Review of Paul Leicester Ford, *The Honorable Peter Sterling.*
76. 51:412 (March, 1883) G. P. Lathrop, Review of Charles M. Clay, *A Modern Hagar.* Sometimes there is at least a hint in Lathrop's and Scudder's reviews that a sense of patriotism is responsible for certain of their reservations. Thus though Scudder praises Henry Adams's *Democracy* as "able," he suggests that it lacks "the quality of higher truthfulness." And he admits, "If we could divest ourselves of our sensitiveness, we should find it easier to praise this book." (46:421-2, September, 1880).
77. 47:707 (May, 1881) H. E. Scudder, Review of George Fleming, *The Head of Medusa.*

78. 62:700 (November, 1888) H. E. Scudder, Review of Mrs. Humphry Ward, *Robert Elsmere.*
79. *Ibid.*
80. 74:273 (August, 1894) H. E. Scudder, Review of Mrs. Humphry Ward, *Marcella.*
81. 78:843 (December, 1896) H. E. Scudder, Review of Mrs. Humphry Ward, *Sir George Tressady.*
82. 69:704-5 (May, 1892) C. T. Copeland, Review of Mrs. Humphry Ward, *The History of David Grieve.*
83. 55:130 (January, 1885) H. E. Scudder, Review of Helen Hunt Jackson, *Ramona.*
84. 45:679 (May, 1880) H. E. Scudder, Review of Jessie Fothergill, *Probation.*
85. 50:710-12 (November, 1882) H. E. Scudder, Review of William Dean Howells, *A Modern Instance.*
86. 56:555 (October, 1885) H. E. Scudder, Review of William Dean Howells, *The Rise of Silas Lapham.*
87. 57:851 (June, 1886) H. E. Scudder, Review of William Dean Howells, *Indian Summer.*
88. 52:704 (November, 1883) H. E. Scudder, Review of William Dean Howells, *A Woman's Reason.*
89. 56:555 (October, 1885) H. E. Scudder, Review of William Dean Howells, *The Rise of Silas Lapham.*
90. 65:564-5 (April, 1890) H. E. Scudder, Review of William Dean Howells, *A Hazard of New Fortunes.*
91. 69:703-4 (May, 1892) H. E. Scudder, Review of William Dean Howells, *The Quality of Mercy.*
92. 80:859 (December, 1897) H. W. Preston, Review of William Dean Howells, *An Open-Eyed Conspiracy.*
93. 74:701 (November, 1894) Sophia Kirk, Review of William Dean Howells, *A Traveler from Altruria.*
94. *Ibid.,* p. 704.
95. 19:553 (May, 1867) E. P. Whipple, "The Genius of Dickens." Whipple remarks that Dickens' "antipathy to malignant natures contrasts strangely with the air of scientific indifference with which Balzac regards them; but it seems to give him more power to penetrate into their souls."
96. 33:695 (June, 1874) G. P. Lathrop, "Growth of the Novel."

Notes

97. 40:382-3 (September, 1877) T. S. Perry, Review of Gustave Flaubert, *Trois Contes*.
98. *Ibid*.
99. 40:294 (September, 1877) Eugene Benson, "A Study of De Stendhal."
100. 37:285 (March, 1876) T. S. Perry, "Victor Cherbuliez." Perry observes that Cherbuliez appeals to the intelligence of his readers but "never touches the heart." (T. S. Perry, Review of Victor Cherbuliez, *L'Idée de Jean Téterol*, 43:548, April, 1879).
101. 40:108 (July, 1877) G. P. Lathrop, Review of Henry James, *The American*.
102. 43:167 (February, 1879) H. W. Preston, Review of Henry James, *The Europeans*.
103. 46:126 (July, 1880) T. S. Perry, Review of Henry James, *Confidence*.
104. 47:710 (May, 1881) H. E. Scudder, Review of Henry James, *Washington Square*.
105. 49:128 (January, 1882) H. E. Scudder, Review of Henry James, *The Portrait of a Lady*.
106. 57:855 (June, 1886) H. E. Scudder, Review of Henry James, *The Bostonians*.
107. 66:422 (September, 1890) H. E. Scudder, Review of Henry James, *The Tragic Muse*.
108. 51:471 (April, 1883) C. D. Warner, "Modern Fiction."
109. 64:530 (October, 1889) Agnes Repplier, "Fiction in the Pulpit." Miss Repplier probably states the case for pleasure more strongly, however, than most *Atlantic* critics. She affirms that it is "not the business of fiction to teach us anything."

Chapter Four

1. See Virginia Harlow, *Thomas Sergeant Perry; a Biography and Letters to Perry from William, Henry, and Garth Wilkinson James* (Durham, 1950).
2. 39:759 (June, 1877) W. D. Howells, Review of Sarah Orne Jewett, *Deephaven*.

Criticism of Fiction

3. 25:505 (April, 1870) W. D. Howells, Review of Björnstjerne Björnson, *Arne, The Happy Boy, The Fisher Maiden.*
4. William Dean Howells, *Criticism and Fiction* (New York, 1891), pp. 15-16.
5. 34:321 (September, 1874) G. P. Lathrop, "The Novel and its Future."
6. 40:108 (July, 1877) G. P. Lathrop, Review of Henry James, *The American.*
7. 50:113 (July, 1882) H. E. Scudder, Review of George Parsons Lathrop, *An Echo of Passion.*
8. 68:568 (October, 1891) H. E. Scudder, Review of William Dean Howells, *Criticism and Fiction.*
9. 55:124 (January, 1885) H. E. Scudder, Review of Charles Egbert Craddock, *Where the Battle was Fought.*
10. 52:706 (November, 1883) H. E. Scudder, Review of Bret Harte, *In the Carquinez Woods.*
11. 50:710 (November, 1882) H. E. Scudder, Review of William Dean Howells, *A Modern Instance.* However, Scudder calls the book "the weightiest novel of the day."
12. 57:856 (June, 1886) H. E. Scudder, Review of William Dean Howells, *Indian Summer.*
13. 54:417 (September, 1884) H. E. Scudder, Review of Edward Bellamy, *Miss Ludington's Sister.* Scudder warns, however, that one does "not secure a reaction against the prevailing mode by a return to antiquated fashions." (Review of Richard D. Blackmore, *Mary Anerly*, 46:826, December, 1880).
14. In his review of *The Tragic Muse,* Scudder suggests that it is that "class of novels, where the judgment of the persons delineated is not emphasized and made unmistakable by a rude confirmation of external circumstances, that is winning the regard of the most thoughtful and penetrating writers," a statement that seems to place him closer to James's views than do certain of his other comments. (66:419, September, 1890).
15. 68:567 (October, 1891) H. E. Scudder, Review of William Dean Howells, *Criticism and Fiction.*
16. W. D. Howells, "The Editor's Study," *Harper's Magazine,* LXXV, 639 (September, 1887).

17. *Ibid.*, LXXVII, 964 (November, 1888).
18. *Ibid.*, LXXVII, 154 (June, 1888).
19. 61:845-6 (June, 1888) H. E. Scudder, Review of Edward Bellamy, *Looking Backward*.
20. Two recent doctoral dissertations give detailed studies of Howells' theories. See Everett Carter, *William Dean Howells' Theory of Realism in Fiction,* University of California, Los Angeles, 1947, and Charles T. Miller, *Howells' Theory of the Novel,* University of Chicago, 1947.
21. 81:142 (January, 1898) H. D. Sedgwick, Jr., Review of Hall Caine, *The Christian*.
22. In an essay in 1895 Charles Miner Thompson calls *Main Traveled Roads* "admirable" but dismisses *Crumbling Idols* as "a foolish book." He insists that Garland "owes his success to the one principle which he shares with the models and masters he despises." ("New Figures in Literature and Art: Hamlin Garland," 76:843, December, 1895).
23. 78:165 (August, 1896) Paul Shorey, "Present Conditions of Literary Production."
24. Norman Foerster has given perhaps the best statement of the range such studies should take. Mr. Foerster writes that we need "studies of the relation between literature and science, not merely the new knowledge, but also the method, the criteria, the temper and attitude, and the effect of these upon idea, form, and style in the various literary *genres* of the period; and particularly the interplay of science with the other motivations of Realism." "The Critical Study of the Victorian Age" in *The Reinterpretation of Victorian Literature,* edited by Joseph E. Baker (Princeton, 1950).
25. See Robert E. Mitchell, unpublished doctoral dissertation, *American Life as Reflected in the Atlantic Monthly, 1857-1881,* Harvard University, 1950.
26. 33:566 (May, 1874) T. S. Perry, "Ivan Turgénieff."
27. F. O. Matthiessen, *Henry James; the Major Phase* (New York, 1944), p. 264.
28. 75:820 (June, 1895) C. M. Thompson, Review of Rowland Robinson, *Danvis Folks*.

29. 69:270 (February, 1892) C. T. Copeland, "The Short Story" [a group of reviews].
30. Max Eastman, *The Literary Mind; its Place in an Age of Science* (New York, 1931), p. 141.
31. The scientist Helmholtz, writing of the lessons that his age had learned from the physical sciences, speaks of both "the absolute, unconditional reverence for facts" and "the effort to detect in all cases relations of cause and effect." Quoted from William Cecil Dampier-Whetham, *A History of Science and its Relations with Philosophy and Religion* (New York, 1931), p. 330.
32. 15:639 (May, 1865) E. P. Whipple, Review of William Makepeace Thackeray, *Vanity Fair*. Whipple suggests, however, that his criticism applies less to *Vanity Fair* than to its successors.
33. 19:549 (May, 1867) E. P. Whipple, "The Genius of Dickens."
34. 1:352 (January, 1858) Ralph Waldo Emerson, "Books."
35. See Note 31 above.
36. 80:511 (October, 1897) H. D. Sedgwick, Jr., "Gabrielle D'Annunzio."
37. 70:403 (September, 1892) Lida Krockow, Review of Friedrich Spielhagen, *Finder und Erfinder*.
38. *Atlantic* criticism has not yet reached the point in which the state of an individual's inner consciousness is of greater interest than his overt acts. However, Sophia Kirk observes with interest Edouard Rod's emphasis on "inward observation" in *Les Trois Coeurs*. Although she finds Rod's experiments more interesting than his finished novel, she grants that theoretically his work is a step "in the right direction," since "much of our existence is passed among imaginary scenes and conversations." (66:279, August, 1890).
39. One is speaking chiefly, of course, of the general textbook accounts. A number of the matters discussed here in regard to form have been noted by Royal A. Gettman in his study *Turgenev in England and America* (Urbana, 1941), and by H. Willard Reninger in an unpublished dissertation, *The Theory and Practice of the American Novel, 1867-1903*, University of Michigan, 1938. Unfortunately, discussions of the

influence of science have often been confined to a reflection of science in subject matter. Among the best studies of this type are Madeleine Cazamian, *Le Roman et les Idées en Angleterre; L'Influence de la Science, 1860-1890* (Paris, 1923) and Leo J. Henkins, *Darwinism in the English Novel, 1860-1910; the Impact of Evolution on Victorian Fiction* (New York, 1940).

40. The issue of dramatic presentation is a complex one. For an interesting study of the problem in certain English writers see Walter C. Phillips, *Dickens, Reade, and Collins: Sensation Writers* (New York, 1919).
41. 33:693 (June, 1874) G. P. Lathrop, "Growth of the Novel."
42. 68:569 (October, 1891) H. E. Scudder, Review of William Dean Howells, *Criticism and Fiction*.
43. For comments on science and religious thinking during the early part of this period see Mitchell, *op. cit.* I am grateful to Mr. Mitchell for discussions on various *Atlantic* problems. His study of science and religion in the *Atlantic* from 1857 to 1881 reveals a keen interest in science and a respect for the scientific method, a slow acceptance of Darwinism perhaps because of Agassiz's opposition, a distrust of Comtian positivism, and a desire to maintain Christian teleology. He suggests that in the Spencerian doctrine of 'purposeful evolution' the *Atlantic* found a satisfactory compromise.
44. Such a view is at least partially confirmed by Frederick William Conner's *Cosmic Optimism; a Study of the Interpretation of Evolution by American Poets from Emerson to Robinson* (Gainesville, Florida, 1949).
45. See Walter Blair, *Native American Humor, 1800-1900* (New York, 1937).
46. 2:896 (December, 1858) G. S. Hillard, Review of R. T. S. Lowell, *The New Priest in Conception Bay*.
47. 4:386 (September, 1859) Review of *High Life in New York*.
48. 19:124 (January, 1867) Review of James Russell Lowell, *The Biglow Papers*.
49. 52:408 (September, 1883) G. P. Lathrop, Review of Mark Twain, *Life on the Mississippi*.

50. 79:499 (April, 1897) C. M. Thompson, "Mark Twain as an Interpreter of American Character."
51. The only mention of Melville's fiction is in an essay "American Sea Songs" by Alfred M. Williams. The article notes in passing that "the novels of Herman Melville, some of the most original in our literature, have given the romance of the South Sea Islands as they appeared to the adventurer of that day; and in Moby-Dick . . . he has shown both the prose and the poetry of a whaling cruise with singular power, although with some touch of extravagance at the end." (69:499, April, 1892).
52. 19:252-3 (February, 1867) W. D. Howells, Review of Herman Melville, *Battle Pieces*.
53. 77:422 (March, 1896) "Comment on New Book."
54. 77:279 (February, 1896) "Comment on New Books."
55. 70:136 (July, 1892) "Comment on New Books."
56. 72:420 (September, 1893) "Comment on New Books."
57. 74:279 (August, 1894) "Comment on New Books."
58. 5:252-3 (February, 1860) James Russell Lowell, Review of Harriet Prescott, *Sir Rohan's Ghost*. Lowell writes, "Criticism in America has reached something like the state of the old Continental currency. There is no honest relation between the promises we make and the specie basis of meaning they profess to represent." He adds that "the *Atlantic* has been and will be sparing in its use of the word genius."
59. Although Perry did not attempt fiction himself, he was an unusually well-read critic and even learned Russian in order to read the great Russian novelists. In fact, Oliver Wendell Holmes called Perry "the best read man I have ever known." Scudder, Lathrop, and Miss Preston all attempted fiction, though Scudder's efforts were limited and Miss Preston's perhaps not very successful. Lathrop, however, received some acclaim from his contemporaries. Howells writes, "Mr. G. P. Lathrop's book is called *Would You Kill Him?* in a lurid taste which we could not sufficiently deplore; but our censure would hardly go beyond the title page. The power which he gave proof of in *An Echo of Passion* is here an intensified force grappling successfully with a more complex

problem, and keeping in the light of common day an action whose springs are in the darkest fastnesses of the soul." "The Editor's Study," *Harper's Magazine,* LXXX, 482 (February, 1890).

60. Parrington, for instance, writes, "Stoddard and Stedman in New York, Boker in Philadelphia, and Aldrich in Boston, stoutly upheld the genteel tradition, of which the *Atlantic Monthly* was the authoritative spokesman." And he adds that "New England parochialism had become a nation-wide nuisance." Vernon Parrington, *Main Currents in American Thought* (New York, 1930), Volume III, 52-3. It should be emphasized, however, that Aldrich does almost no critical writing on fiction in the *Atlantic*.

61. 1:351 (January, 1858) Ralph Waldo Emerson, "Books." Though Emerson is at his weakest as a critic of fiction—see the present writer's M.A. thesis, *Emerson's Criticism of American Literature,* Iowa, 1942—his prediction that the novel "will find the way to our interiors one day and will not always be the novel of costume merely" is a rather happy characterization of the development of fiction during this period.

62. James's relation to the *Atlantic* is an interesting one. In addition to several critical essays and a number of short stories, his contributions to the magazine include *Roderick Hudson, The American, The Europeans, The Portrait of a Lady, The Princess Casamassima, The Tragic Muse,* and *The Spoils of Poynton* [published serially as *The Old Things*]. Certain objections to James's work have already been pointed out. There is, however, frequent praise for his style. Lathrop calls him "a unique and versatile writer of acute power and great brilliancy of performance." (Review of *Roderick Hudson,* 37:238, February, 1876). Howells speaks of *A Passionate Pilgrim and Other Tales* as "a marvel of delightful workmanship." (35:490, April, 1875). Scudder prefers James's novels to his short stories but he admits, "Nevertheless, he remains today, in some respects, the consummate artist in miniature story-telling of this generation." (Review of *The Real Thing and Other Tales,* 72:695, November, 1893).

63. Howells quotes with approval James's comment on morality, that "it is in reality simply a part of the essential richness of inspiration,—it has nothing to do with the artistic process, and it has everything to do with the artistic effect." "That," says Howells, "is almost the best thing in this superior book. The point has hardly been put with so much grasp and cleverness before." (Review of *French Poets and Novelists,* 42:119, July, 1878). And it is certainly true that James formulates other policies with a similar "grasp and cleverness."
64. 34:322 (September, 1874) G. P. Lathrop, "The Novel and its Future."
65. Herbert J. Muller, *Modern Fiction, A Study of Values* (New York, 1937), p. 46.
66. Van Meter Ames, "The Novel: Between Art and Science," *Kenyon Review,* V (Winter, 1943), 34-48.
67. The phrase forms the title of a chapter on the Stedman-Aldrich group in *Literary History of the United States,* Vol. II (New York, 1948).
68. Again the phrase is from a chapter title. Bernard Smith in *Forces in American Criticism* (New York, 1939) uses it to characterize E. P. Whipple and others.

REGISTER OF REVIEWS AND CRITICAL ESSAYS

The following pages give a chronological listing of the articles and reviews in the *Atlantic* from 1857 to 1898 which deal either directly or indirectly with fiction. In order to give as full a picture of literary taste during the period as possible, articles which are chiefly biographical in nature are also listed. Reviews are indicated by an asterisk. Names of reviewers—wherever it has been possible to identify them through the *Atlantic Index* and the *Atlantic Index Supplement*—are given in parentheses. Initials have been used to designate the most frequent contributors of critical notices: James Russell Lowell, Edwin Percy Whipple, Thomas Wentworth Higginson, William Dean Howells, Thomas Sergeant Perry, George Parsons Lathrop, Harriet Waters Preston, Charles T. Copeland, and Horace E. Scudder. Each entry has been numbered to allow for indexing.

1. 1:123 (November, 1857) Charles Reade, *White Lies.**
2. 1:254-5 (December, 1857) Henri Monnier, *Mémoires de M. Joseph Prudhomme.**
3. 1:255-6 (December, 1857) Otto Ludwig, *Thüringer Naturen, Charakter und Sittenbilder in Erzählungen.**
4. 1:384 (January, 1858) Robert Heller, *Der Reichspostreiter in Ludwigsburg.**
5. 1:638-9 (March, 1858) F. D. Guerrazzi, *Beatrice Cenci,* translation* (J. R. L.)
6. 1:888-9 (May, 1858) Sir Walter Scott, *Waverly Novels,* Household edition.*
7. 1:891-2 (May, 1858) George Eliot, *Scenes of Clerical Life.**

8. 1:892 (May, 1858) Anna Cora Ritchie, *Twin Roses*.*
9. 2:896-9 (December, 1858) R. T. S. Lowell, *The New Priest in Conception Bay** (G. S. Hillard).
10. 3:133 (January, 1859) *Vernon Grove; or Hearts as They Are*.*
11. 3:136 (January, 1859) *Ernest Carroll; or Artist Life in Italy*.*
12. 3:652 (May, 1859) B. F. Presbury, *The Mustee; or Love and Liberty*.*
13. 3:693-703 (June, 1859) W. Sargent, "Some Inedited Memorials of Smollett."
14. 4:129-31 (July, 1859) Charles Reade, *Love Me Little, Love Me Long*.*
15. 4:131-2 (July, 1859) J. W. De Forest, *Seacliff; or The Mystery of the Westervelts*.*
16. 4:385-6 (September, 1859) *High Life in New York*.*
17. 4:394-5 (September, 1859) F. H. Underwood, "The Novels of James Fenimore Cooper."
18. 4:521-2 (October, 1859) George Eliot, *Adam Bede*.*
19. 4:648-50 (November, 1859) *Out of the Depths; the Story of a Woman's Life*.*
20. 4:774-5 (December, 1859) *Sword and Gown*.*
21. 5:123 (January, 1860) Thomas Hughes, *Tom Brown at Oxford*.*
22. 5:252-4 (February, 1860) H. E. Prescott, *Sir Rohan's Ghost** (J. R. L.).
23. 5:381-2 (March, 1860) Charles Reade, *A Good Fight and Other Tales** (E. H. House).
24. 5:506-7 (April, 1860) Miss Pardoe, *The Adopted Heir*.*
25. 5:507 (April, 1860) Ernest Feydeau, *Fanny*, translation.*
26. 5:509-10 (April, 1860) Nathaniel Hawthorne, *The Marble Faun** (J. R. L.).
27. 5:511 (April, 1860) T. S. Arthur, *Twenty Years Ago and Now*.*
28. 5:614-22 (May, 1860) E. P. Whipple, "Nathaniel Hawthorne."
29. 5:638 (May, 1860) *Mary Staunton; or The Pupils of Marvel Hall*.*
30. 5:638 (May, 1860) E. L. Llewellyn, *Title Hunting*.*

31. 5:754-5 (June, 1860) *Mademoiselle Mori; a Tale of Modern Rome** (Charles Eliot Norton).
32. 5:756-7 (June, 1860) George Eliot, *The Mill on the Floss.**
33. 6:119-20 (July, 1860) Maria Cummins, *El Furedis** (E. P. W.).
34. 6:121-3 (July, 1860) Elizabeth Wetherell, *Say and Seal** (F. C. Hopkinson).
35. 6:123-4 (July, 1860) A. S. Roe, *How Could He Help It; or The Heart Triumphant.**
36. 6:129-41 (August, 1860) W. L. Symonds, "The Carnival of the Romantic."
37. 6:376-7 (September, 1860) J. T. Trowbridge, *The Old Battle Ground** (J. R. L.).
38. 6:601-12 (November, 1860) G. Putnam, "Recollections of Irving."
39. 6:637 (November, 1860) Honoré de Balzac, *Sketches of Parisian Life** *The Greatness and Decline of Cesar Birotteau*, translation.*
40. 7:125-6 (January, 1861) J. G. Holland, *Miss Gilbert's Career** (J. R. L.).
41. 7:383-4 (March, 1861) *Harrington.**
42. 7:509-11 (April, 1861) Oliver Wendell Holmes, *Elsie Venner** (J. R. L.).
43. 7:639 (May, 1861) Charles Dickens, *Works,* Household edition.*
44. 8:242-51 (August, 1861) G. W. Curtis, "Theodore Winthrop."
45. 8:380-2 (September, 1861) Charles Dickens, *Great Expectations** (E. P. W.).
46. 8:382-3 (September, 1861) Thomas Hughes, *Tom Brown at Oxford.**
47. 8:513-34 (November, 1861) J. W. Howe, "George Sand."
48. 8:773-5 (December, 1861) Theodore Winthrop, *Cecil Dreeme** (E. P. W.)
49. 9:52-68 (January, 1862) G. S. Hillard, "James Fenimore Cooper."
50. 9:270-1 (February, 1862) Charles Reade, *The Cloister and the Hearth** (E. P. W.).

51. 9:520-1 (April, 1862) Theodore Winthrop, *John Brent**
    (E. P. W.).
52. 9:525-6 (April, 1862) Gustave Merlet, *Le Réalisme et la Fantaisie dans la Littérature.**
53. 9:653 (May, 1862) Charles Dickens, *Martin Chuzzlewit,* Household edition.*
54. 9:763-75 (June, 1862) H. E. Prescott, "The Author of 'Charles Auchester'" [Elizabeth Sheppard].
55. 10:124-5 (July, 1862) Victor Hugo, *Les Misérables—Fantine** (E. P. W.).
56. 10:126-8 (July, 1862) Harriet Beecher Stowe, *The Pearl of Orr's Island** (E. P. W.).
57. 10:251-2 (August, 1862) Henry Kingsley, *Ravenshoe.**
58. 10:498-502 (October, 1862) S. Conyers, "Elizabeth Sara Sheppard."
59. 10:646-8 (November, 1862) Pierre M. Irving, *The Life and Letters of Washington Irving** (G. S. Hillard).
60. 11:136-9 (January, 1863) J. P. Richter, *Titan,* translation* (J. Weiss).
61. 11:235-40 (February, 1863) A. M. Waterston, "Jane Austen."
62. 12:153-9 (August, 1863) C. Nordhoff, "Theodore Winthrop's Writings."
63. 12:685-701 (December, 1863) "Literary Life in Paris."
64. 13:126-8 (January, 1864) Epes Sargeant, *Peculiar; a Tale of the Great Transition.**
65. 13:132-5 (January, 1864) Bayard Taylor, *Hannah Thurston; a Story of American Life** (M. A. Dodge).
66. 13:371-9 (March, 1864) Bayard Taylor, "William Makepeace Thackeray."
67. 13:694-701 (June, 1864) D. G. Mitchell, "Washington Irving."
68. 14:98-101 (July, 1864) O. W. Holmes, "Hawthorne."
69. 14:137-49 (August, 1864) H. E. Prescott, "Charles Reade."
70. 14:254-6 (August, 1864) Anthony Trollope, *The Small House at Allington.**
71. 14:292-303 (September, 1864) J. D. Osborn, "Literary Life in Paris."

Register of Reviews and Critical Essays

72. 14:515-17 (October, 1864) Harriet E. Prescott, *Azarian** (T. W. H.).
73. 14:660-71 (December, 1864) Kate Field, "English Authors in Florence."
74. 15:378 (March, 1865) Margaret Hosmer, *The Morrisons, a Story of Domestic Life** (T. W. H.).
75. 15:378-9 (March, 1865) Jean Ingelow, *Studies for Stories** (T. W. H.).
76. 15:639-40 (May, 1865) William Makepeace Thackeray, *Vanity Fair** (E. P. W.).
77. 16:121 (July, 1865) Henry Kingsley, *The Hillyars and the Burtons.**
78. 16:121 (July, 1865) *Christian's Mistake.**
79. 16:121 (July, 1865) J. S. Le Fanu, *Uncle Silas.**
80. 16:273-82 (September, 1885) D. A. Wasson, "Wilhelm Meister's Apprenticeship."
81. 16:356-9 (September, 1865) Mrs. John Farrar, "A Visit to the Edgeworths."
82. 16:448-57 (October, 1865) D. A. Wasson, "Wilhelm Meister's Apprenticeship," Part II.
83. 16:510-12 (October, 1865) J. P. Richter, *Hesperus, or Forty-five Dog Post Days,* translation* (J. Weiss).
84. 17:246-8 (February, 1866) E. Foxton, *Herman; or, Young Knighthood** (M. A. Dodge).
85. 17:384 (March, 1866) Mrs. Charles, *Winifred Bertram and the World She Lived In** (T. W. H.).
86. 17:525 (April, 1866) Meta Lander, *Esperance** (T. W. H.).
87. 17:650 (May, 1866) *A Noble Life.**
88. 17:775-8 (June, 1866) Bayard Taylor, *The Story of Kennett** (W. D. H.).
89. 18:128 (July, 1866) *Fifteen Days; an Extract from Edward Colvil's Journal** (W. D. H.).
90. 18:256 (August, 1866) Joseph von Eichendorff, *Memoirs of a Good for Nothing.**
91. 18:381-2 (September, 1866) Wilkie Collins, *Armadale.**
92. 18:479-92 (October, 1866) Henry James, "The Novels of George Eliot."

141

Criticism of Fiction

93. 18:645 (November, 1866) George F. Harrington, *Inside; a Chronicle of Secession.**
94. 18:767-9 (December, 1866) Charles Reade, *Griffith Gaunt; or Jealousy** (W. D. H.).
95. 19:546-54 (May, 1867) E. P. Whipple, "The Genius of Dickens."
96. 20:120-2 (July, 1867) J. W. De Forest, *Miss Ravenel's Conversion from Secession to Loyalty** (W. D. H.).
97. 20:123-4 (July, 1867) C. H. Webb, *Liffith Lank, or Lunacy* St. Twel'mo.**
98. 20:124-5 (July, 1867) William K. Paulding, *The Literary Life of James K. Paulding** (W. D. H.).
99. 20:476-84 (October, 1867) H. T. Tuckerman, "The Writings of T. Adolphus Trollope."
100. 21:128 (January, 1868) Bret Harte, *Condensed Novels and other Papers.**
101. 21:382 (March, 1868) Sidney Lanier, *Tiger Lilies.**
102. 21:664-71 (June, 1868) Eugene Benson, "Théophile Gautier, a Literary Artist."
103. 21:761-4 (June, 1868) Henry Ward Beecher, *Norwood; or Village Life in New England** (W. D. H.).
104. 22:255 (August, 1868) Charles Reade and Dion Boucicault, *Foul Play** (W. D. H.).
105. 22:359-74 (September, 1868) E. P. Peabody, "The Genius of Hawthorne."
106. 22:634-5 (November, 1868) E. E. Hale, *If, Yes, and Perhaps; Four Possibilities and Six Exaggerations, with Some Bits of Fact** (W. D. H.).
107. 22:637 (November, 1868) Annie L. McGregor, *John Ward's Governess.**
108. 22:762-4 (December, 1868) Charles Dickens, *A Christmas Carol.**
109. 23:134-5 (January, 1869) Anna E. Dickinson, *What Answer?** (W. D. H.).
110. 23:387-8 (March, 1869) Charles Nordhoff, *Cape Cod and All Along the Shore.**
111. 23:762-4 (June, 1869) Berthold Auerbach, *Edelweiss,* translation* (W. D. H.).

Register of Reviews and Critical Essays

112. 23:767-8 (June, 1869) Victor Rydberg, *The Last Athenian,* translation* (W. D. H.).
113. 24:259 (August, 1869) Richard Henry Dana, *Two Years Before the Mast* (W. D. H.).
114. 24:764-6 (December, 1869) Samuel Clemens, *The Innocents Abroad* (W. D. H.).
115. 25:56-63 (January, 1870) Thomas Wentworth Higginson, "Americanism in Literature."
116. 25:124-5 (January, 1870) Thomas Bailey Aldrich, *The Story of a Bad Boy* (W. D. H.).
117. 25:247-8 (February, 1870) William Makepeace Thackeray, *Miscellanies* *Catherine* (W. D. H.).
118. 25:504-12 (April, 1870) Björnstjerne Björnson, *Arne* *The Happy Boy* *The Fisher Maiden* (W. D. H.).
119. 25:512 (April, 1870) *Red as a Rose is She**
120. 25:633-5 (May, 1870) Bret Harte, *The Luck of Roaring Camp, and Other Stories* (W. D. H.).
121. 25:756-7 (June, 1870) Elizabeth Stuart Phelps, *Hedged In.**
122. 25:762-3 (June, 1870) Berriedale, *Unforgiven.**
123. 25:763 (June, 1870) Justice McCarthy, *My Enemy's Daughter.**
124. 26:128 (July, 1870) Mrs. C. A. Steele, *So Runs the World Away.**
125. 26:195-9 (August, 1870) E. P. Whipple, "Mr. Hardhack on the Sensational in Literature and Life."
126. 26:235-45 (August, 1870) J. T. Fields, "Some Memories of Charles Dickens."
127. 26:249-51 (August, 1870) Benjamin Disraeli, *Lothair* (Henry James).
128. 26:256 (August, 1870) Hawley Smart, *A Race for a Wife.**
129. 26:257-72 (September, 1870) G. S. Hillard, "The English Notebooks of Nathaniel Hawthorne."
130. 26:381 (September, 1870) James De Mille, *The Lady of the Ice.**
131. 26:382 (September, 1870) Ruffini, *Carlino.**
132. 26:383-4 (September, 1870) Hans Christian Andersen, *O.T.; A Danish Romance* (W. D. H.).

143

133. 26:384 (September, 1870) John Franklin Swift, *Robert Greathouse.**
134. 26:384 (September, 1870) Hawley Smart, *Breezie Langton.**
135. 26:476-82 (October, 1870) G. W. Putnam, "Four Months with Charles Dickens."
136. 26:504-6 (October, 1870) William M. Baker, *The New Timothy** (W. D. H.).
137. 26:509-10 (October, 1870) Frank Lee Benedict, *Miss Van Kortland** (Ralph Keeler).
138. 26:591-9 (November, 1870) G. W. Putnam, "Four Months with Charles Dickens," Part II.
139. 26:632-4 (November, 1870) Hans Christian Andersen, *Only a Fiddler** (W. D. H.).
140. 26:636-7 (November, 1870) Friedrich Spielhagen, *Hammer and Anvil** (Ralph Keeler).
141. 26:637-8 (November, 1870) M. Goldschmidt, *The Flying Mail** (W. D. H.).
142. 26:637-8 (November, 1870) Magdalen Thoreson, *Old Olaf.**
143. 26:637-8 (November, 1870) Björnstjerne Björnson, *The Railroad and the Churchyard.**
144. 26:759-60 (December, 1870) Ralph Keeler, *Vagabond Adventures** (W. D. H.).
145. 26:760 (December, 1870) George Sand, *Monsieur Sylvestre.**
146. 26:761-3 (December, 1870) Christian Reid, *Valerie Aylmer.**
147. 27:122-37 (January, 1871) J. T. Fields, "Our Whispering Gallery" [Thackeray].
148. 27:144 (January, 1871) Sylvester Judd, *Margaret** (W. D. H.).
149. 27:246-57 (February, 1871) J. T. Fields, "Our Whispering Gallery" [Hawthorne].
150. 27:265-7 (February, 1871) Alexis Pisemski, *Tausend Seelen** (T. S. P.).
151. 27:380-92 (March, 1871) J. T. Fields, "Our Whispering Gallery" [Hawthorne].
152. 27:504-12 (April, 1871) J. T. Fields, "Our Whispering Gallery" [Hawthorne].
153. 27:524 (April, 1871) Julian Schmidt, *Bilder aus dem geistigen Leben unserer Zeit** (T. S. P.).

Register of Reviews and Critical Essays

154. 27:639-53 (May, 1871) J. T. Fields, "Our Whispering Gallery" [Hawthorne].
155. 27:763-71 (June, 1871) J. T. Fields, "Our Whispering Gallery" [Dickens].
156. 28:106-14 (July, 1871) J. T. Fields, "Our Whispering Gallery" [Dickens].
157. 28:126 (July, 1871) Caroline Chesebro', *The Foe in the Household.**
158. 28:222-31 (August, 1871) J. T. Fields, "Our Whispering Gallery" [Dickens].
159. 28:248-51 (August, 1871) Gustave Droz, *Around a Spring** (Henry James).
160. 28:254-5 (August, 1871) Katherine Valerio, *Ina.**
161. 28:256 (August, 1871) Bret Harte, *Condensed Novels.**
162. 28:358-71 (September, 1871) J. T. Fields, "Our Whispering Gallery" [Dickens].
163. 28:377-8 (September, 1871) Harriet Beecher Stowe, *Pink and White Tyranny** (W. D. H.).
164. 28:379-81 (September, 1871) Hans Christian Andersen, *The Story of my Life.** (W. D. H.).
165. 28:383-4 (September, 1871) Charles Reade, *A Terrible Temptation** (W. D. H.).
166. 28:432-3 (October, 1871) T. W. Higginson, "An Evening with Mrs. Hawthorne."
167. 28:501-10 (October, 1871) J. T. Fields, "Our Whispering Gallery" [Dickens].
168. 28:624-33 (November, 1871) J. T. Fields, "Our Whispering Gallery" [Dickens].
169. 28:750-58 (December, 1871) J. T. Fields, "Our Whispering Gallery" [Miss Mitford].
170. 29:110 (January, 1872) Mrs. A. D. T. Whitney, *Real Folks.**
171. 29:110-11 (January, 1872) Harriet Beecher Stowe, *My Wife and I.**
172. 29:111 (January, 1872) J. W. De Forest, *Overland.**
173. 29:113 (January, 1872) Victor Cherbuliez, *La Revanche de Joseph Noirel** (T. S. P.).
174. 29:114 (January, 1872) Ivan Turgénieff, *Helena** (T. S. P.).

175. 29:114 (January, 1872) Julian Schmidt, *Bilder aus dem geistigen Leben unserer Zeit,* neue Folge.*
176. 29:239-41 (February, 1872) John Forster, *The Life of Charles Dickens,* Vol. I* (W. D. H.).
177. 29:243 (February, 1872) Karl Gutzkow, *Fritz Ellrodt** (T. S. P.).
178. 29:243 (February, 1872) M. Gaborian, *La Clique Dorée** (T. S. P.).
179. 29:363-4 (March, 1872) Edward Eggleston, *The Hoosier Schoolmaster** (W. D. H.).
180. 29:364-5 (March, 1872) J. W. De Forest, *Kate Beaumont** (W. D. H.).
181. 29:365-6 (March, 1872) Harriet Beecher Stowe, *Oldtown Fireside Stories.**
182. 29:366 (March, 1872) Mrs. Annie Edwards, *Ought We to Visit Her?**
183. 29:366 (March, 1872) Mrs. Sidney S. Harris, *Richard Vandermarck.**
184. 29:498 (April, 1872) J. T. Fields, *Yesterdays with Authors** (W. D. H.).
185. 29:624-6 (May, 1872) *Passages from the French and Italian Notebooks of Nathaniel Hawthorne** (W. D. H.).
186. 29:626 (May, 1872) Harriet Prescott Spofford, *Thief in the Night.**
187. 29:628 (May, 1872) Erckmann-Chatrian, *L'Histoire du Plébiscite** (T. S. P.).
188. 29:630 (May, 1872) Jonas Lie, *Den Fremsynte, eller Billeder fra Nordland.**
189. 29:751 (June, 1872) Bayard Taylor, *Beauty and the Beast and Tales of Home.**
190. 29:754 (June, 1872) Samuel Clemens, *Roughing It** (W. D. H.).
191. 30:117 (July, 1872) James De Mille, *The American Baron.**
192. 30:117-18 (July, 1872) C. d'Héricault, *Thermidor; Paris en 1794.**
193. 30:118 (July, 1872) Octave Feuillet, *Julie de Trécoeur.**
194. 30:243-4 (August, 1872) Ivan Turgénieff, *Smoke,* translation (W. D. H.).*

195. 30:370 (September, 1872) George Sand, *Francia** (T. S. P.).
196. 30:370 (September, 1872) Adolphe Joanne, *Albert Fleurier** (T. S. P.).
197. 30:452-60 (October, 1872) G. P. Lathrop, "History of Hawthorne's Last Romance."
198. 30:487-8 (October, 1872) William Flagg, *A Good Investment; a Story of the Upper Ohio*.*
199. 30:491-2 (October, 1872) Florence Montgomery, *Thrown Together*.*
200. 30:495 (October, 1872) Gustave Droz, *Babolain** (T. S. P.).
201. 30:629 (November, 1872) *The Rose Garden*.*
202. 30:630-1 (November, 1872) Ivan Turgénieff, *Frühlingsfluthen** (T. S. P.).
203. 30:746-7 (December, 1872) Edward Eggleston, *The End of the World** (W. D. H.).
204. 31:105 (January, 1873) Victor Cherbuliez, *Joseph Noirel's Revenge** (W. D. H.).
205. 31:107 (January, 1873) Mary Healy, *A Summer's Romance*.*
206. 31:109 (January, 1873) James De Mille, *A Comedy of Terrors*.*
207. 31:110-11 (January, 1873) Otto Glagau, *Die Russiche Literatur und Iwan Turgenjew*.*
208. 31:112 (January, 1873) Ivan Turgénieff, *Der Oberst** *Der Fatalist** *The Lear of the Steppe** (T. S. P.).
209. 31:113 (January, 1873) George Sand, *Nanon** (T. S. P.).
210. 31:237-8 (February, 1873) John Forster, *The Life of Charles Dickens*, Vol. II* (W. D. H.).
211. 31:239 (February, 1873) Ivan Turgénieff, *Liza** (W. D. H.).
212. 31:243 (February, 1873) Nikolai Gogol, *Tarass Boulba**
213. 31:358-9 (March, 1873) Jean Ingelow, *Off the Skelligs*.*
214. 31:359 (March, 1873) J. T. Trowbridge, *Coupon Bonds and Other Stories*.*
215. 31:490-4 (April, 1873) George Eliot, *Middlemarch** (A. G. Sedgwick).
216. 31:626 (May, 1873) George Bryant Woods, *Essays, Sketches, and Stories*.*
217. 31:750 (June, 1873) W. S. Mayo, *Never Again*.*
218. 32:116-17 (July, 1873) Wilhelm Bergsöe, *Bruden fra Rörvig*.*

219. 32:239-40 (August, 1873) Ivan Turgénieff, *On the Eve**
(G. P. L.).
220. 32:369-70 (September, 1873) Ivan Turgénieff, *Dmitrine Roudine** (W. D. H.).
221. 32:371 (September, 1873) Miss Thackeray [Mrs. Richmond Ritchie], *Old Kensington** (G. P. L.).
222. 32:375-6 (September, 1873) Harriet W. Preston, *Love in the Nineteenth Century** (W. D. H.).
223. 32:500-1 (October, 1873) Thomas Hardy, *A Pair of Blue Eyes.**
224. 32:501 (October, 1873) Charles Reade, *A Simpleton.**
225. 32:501-4 (October, 1873) Victor Cherbuliez, *Meta Holdenis** (T. S. P.).
226. 32:611-21 (November, 1873) Clarence Gordon, "Mr. De Forest's Novels."
227. 32:625-6 (November, 1873) T. B. Aldrich, *Marjorie Daw and Other People** (W. D. H.).
228. 32:638 (November, 1873) Julian Schmidt, *Neue Bilder aus dem geistigen Leben unserer Zeit*, III*
229. 32:641-55 (December, 1873) L. J. Jennings, "Disraeli."
230. 32:746-7 (December, 1873) Dr. Charles Smart, *Driven from the Path.**
231. 32:747 (December, 1873) Leonard Kip, *The Dead Marquise.**
232. 32:747-8 (December, 1873) Henry Peterson, *Pemberton.**
233. 32:754-6 (December, 1873) C. Potvin, *De la Corruption Littéraire en France** (T. S. P.).
234. 33:108-10 (January, 1874) T. W. Higginson, *Oldport Days** (C. P. Cranch).
235. 33:110-11 (January, 1874) Robertson Gray, *Brave Hearts.**
236. 33:366-7 (March, 1874) W. D. Howells, "Ralph Keeler."
237. 33:485-8 (April, 1874) E. S. Nadal, "The British Upper Classes in Fiction."
238. 33:497 (April, 1874) Victor Cherbuliez, *Prosper Randoce** (T. S. P.).
239. 33:565-75 (May, 1874) T. S. Perry, "Ivan Turgénieff."
240. 33:616-17 (May, 1874) Edward Bulwer, Lord Lytton, *The Parisians.**

241. 33:617-18 (May, 1874) Anthony Trollope, *Phineas Redux** (T. S. P.).
242. 33:618-19 (May, 1874) Mrs. Alexander, *The Wooing o't** (Mrs. Zina Fay Pierce).
243. 33:619 (May, 1874) T. A. Trollope, *Diamond Cut Diamond.**
244. 33:621-2 (May, 1874) John Forster, *The Life of Charles Dickens,* III* (W. D. H.).
245. 33:627-9 (May, 1874) Victor Hugo, *Quatrevingt-treize** (T. S. P.).
246. 33:684-97 (June, 1874) G. P. Lathrop, "Growth of the Novel."
247. 33:745 (June, 1874) Edward Eggleston, *The Circuit Rider** (W. D. H.).
248. 33:747 (June, 1874) *Thorpe Regis** (T. S. P.).
249. 34:115 (July, 1874) Rebecca Harding Davis, *John Andross** (T. S. P.).
250. 34:227-9 (August, 1874) T. B. Aldrich, *Prudence Palfrey** (W. D. H.).
251. 34:229 (August, 1874) J. W. De Forest, *The Wetherel Affair** (W. D. H.).
252. 34:230 (August, 1874) William M. Baker, *Mose Evans** (W. D. H.).
253. 34:230-1 (August, 1874) Louise Chandler Moulton, *Some Women's Hearts** (G. P. L.).
254. 34:231 (August, 1874) Ivan Turgénieff, *Spring Floods,* translation*
255. 34:231 (August, 1874) John Esten Cooke, *Pretty Mrs. Gaston and Other Stories** (H. W. P. with L. P. Dodge).
256. 34:231 (August, 1874) Thomas Hardy, *Desperate Remedies.**
257. 34:241-3 (August, 1874) Gustave Flaubert, *La Tentation de Saint Antoine** (T. S. P.).
258. 34:313-24 (September, 1874) G. P. Lathrop, "The Novel and Its Future."
259. 34:361 (September, 1874) Frank Lee Benedict, *John Worthington's Name** (T. S. P.).
260. 34:362-3 (September, 1874) F. H. Underwood, *Lord of Himself** (W. D. H.).

Criticism of Fiction

261. 34:372-3 (September, 1874) Le Comte de Gobineau, *Les Pléiades** (T. S. P.).
262. 34:433-40 (October, 1874) T. S. Perry, "Berthold Auerbach."
263. 34:493 (October, 1874) Christian Reid, *A Daughter of Bohemia** (T. S. P.).
264. 34:624-5 (November, 1874) H. H. Boyesen, *Gunnar** (W. D. H.).
265. 34:746-8 (December, 1874) Julian Hawthorne, *Idolatry** (Henry James).
266. 34:748-9 (December, 1874) E. P. Roe, *Opening a Chestnut Burr** (H. W. P.).
267. 34:749 (December, 1874) Henry Churton, *Toinette** (H. W. P.).
268. 35:36-41 (January, 1875) T. S. Perry, "Fritz Reuter."
269. 35:107-8 (January, 1875) Adelaide Trafton, *Katherine Earle.**
270. 35:108 (January, 1875) W. L. M. Jay, *Holden with the Cords.**
271. 35:108-9 (January, 1875) D. R. Castleton, *Salem: a Tale of the Seventeenth Century.**
272. 35:238 (February, 1875) J. W. De Forest, *Honest John Vane.**
273. 35:247-8 (February, 1875) Louise von Francois, *Die letze Reckenbürgerin** (T. S. P.).
274. 35:373 (March, 1875) Camille Lemonnier, *Contes Flamonds et Wallons** (T. S. P.).
275. 35:490-5 (April, 1875) Henry James, *A Passionate Pilgrim and Other Tales** (W. D. H.).
276. 35:505 (April, 1875) Julian Schmidt, *Bilder aus dem geistigen Leben unserer Zeit** (T. S. P.).
277. 35:623 (May, 1875) Christian Reid, *Hearts and Hands.**
278. 35:623 (May, 1875) Mrs. J. H. Ridell, *Too Much Alone.**
279. 35:623-4 (May, 1875) Mrs. K. S. Macquoid, *My Story.**
280. 35:627-8 (May, 1875) B. L. Farjeon, *At the Sign of the Silver Flagon.**
281. 35:628 (May, 1875) J. S. Le Fanu, *Checkmate.**
282. 35:628 (May, 1875) Mary Cowden Clarke, *A Rambling Story.**

283. 35:628-9 (May, 1875) Gustave Droz, *Une Femme Gênante** (T. S. P.).
284. 35:629 (May, 1875) Victor Cherbuliez, *Miss Rovel.**
285. 35:736-7 (June, 1875) Constance Fenimore Woolson, *Castle Nowhere** (W. D. H.).
286. 35:748-9 (June, 1875) Iwan Turgenjew, *Skizzen aus dem Tagebuche eines Jägers** German translation (T. S. P.).
287. 36:111-12 (July, 1875) Frank Lee Benedict, *Mr. Vaughan's Heir** (T. S. P.).
288. 36:167-74 (August, 1875) T. S. Perry, "Victor Hugo."
289. 36:248 (August, 1875) Harriet Beecher Stowe, *We and Our Neighbors** (G. P. L.).
290. 36:363 (September, 1875) Hjalmar Hjorth Boyesen, *A Norseman's Pilgrimage** (G. P. L.).
291. 36:505 (October, 1875) Ivan Turgénieff, *Punin and Baburin** *Die Lebendige Mumie** (T. S. P.).
292. 36:506 (October, 1875) Berthold Auerbach, *Drei einzige Töchter** (T. S. P.).
293. 36:598-602 (November, 1875) Horace E. Scudder, "Andersen's Short Stories."
294. 36:630 (November, 1875) Helen King Spangler, *The Physician's Wife** (T. S. P.).
295. 36:749-50 (December, 1875) Mark Twain, *Sketches** (W. D. H.).
296. 36:759-60 (December, 1875) Gustave Droz, *Les Étangs** (T. S. P.).
297. 37:117-18 (January, 1876) J. G. Holland, *Sevenoaks** (G. P. L.).
298. 37:237-8 (February, 1876) Henry James, *Roderick Hudson** (G. P. L.).
299. 37:238-9 (February, 1876) J. W. De Forest, *Playing the Mischief** (G. P. L.).
300. 37:239 (February, 1876) Madame Augustus Craven, *Jettatrice** or *The Veil Withdrawn** (T. S. P.).
301. 37:239 (February, 1876) Henry Kingsley, *Stretton.**
302. 37:270-87 (March, 1876) T. S. Perry, "Victor Cherbuliez."
303. 37:378 (March, 1876) Theo Gift, *Pretty Miss Bellow** (H. W. P. with L. P. Dodge).

304. 37:379-80 (March, 1876) Lal Behari Day, *Govinda Samanta**
 (T. S. P.).
305. 37:404-11 (April, 1876) G. P. Lathrop, "Early American Novelists."
306. 37:607-616 (May, 1876) Hjalmar Hjorth Boyesen, "Literary Aspects of the Romantic School."
307. 37:621-2 (May, 1876) Mark Twain, *The Adventures of Tom Sawyer** (W. D. H.).
308. 37:751-2 (June, 1876) Charles Henry Jones, *Davault's Mills.**
309. 38:219-24 (August, 1876) E. P. Whipple, "Dickens and *The Pickwick Papers.*"
310. 38:244 (August, 1876) Thomas Hardy, *The Hand of Ethelberta** (G. P. L.).
311. 38:244-5 (August, 1876) Peter Pennot, *Achsah: A New England Life Study.**
312. 38:245-6 (August, 1876) Anthony Trollope, *The Prime Minister** (G. P. L.).
313. 38:248-9 (August, 1876) Alphonse Daudet, *Froment Jeune et Risler Aîné** (T. S. P.).
314. 38:250 (August, 1876) Alphonse Daudet, *Jack** (T. S. P.).
315. 38:368 (September, 1876) Mary Mapes Dodge, *Theophilus and Others.**
316. 38:368 (September, 1876) Susan and Anna Warner, *Wych Hazel.**
317. 38:371 (September, 1876) Charles Deslys, *Le Serment de Madeleine** (T. S. P.).
318. 38:444-51 (October, 1876) T. S. Perry, "George Sand."
319. 38:474-79 (October, 1876) E. P. Whipple, "*Oliver Twist.*"
320. 38:684-94 (December, 1876) Henry James, "*Daniel Deronda*: a Conversation."
321. 39:243-4 (February, 1877) [Helen Hunt Jackson], *Mercy Philbrick's Choice** (H. W. P.).
322. 39:244 (February, 1877) Hjalmar Hjorth Boyesen, *Tales from Two Hemispheres** (G. P. L.).
323. 39:248-9 (February, 1877) Erich Schmidt, *Richardson, Rousseau, und Goethe** (T. S. P.).
324. 39:353-8 (March, 1877) E. P. Whipple, "Dickens's *Hard Times.*"

325. 39:370 (March, 1877) E. E. Hale, *Philip Nolan's Friends** (G. P. L.).
326. 39:370-1 (March, 1877) Susan and Anna Warner, *The Gold of Chickaree** (T. S. P.).
327. 39:373 (March, 1877) *The Jericho Road: a Story of Western Life*.*
328. 39:373-4 (March, 1877) *Student Life at Harvard** (T. S. P.).
329. 39:381 (March, 1877) *Un Coin du Monde** (T. S. P.).
330. 39:498-500 (April, 1877) Rosmus Andersen, *Viking Tales of the North*, translation.*
331. 39:500 (April, 1877) Bret Harte, *Thankful Blossom** (G. P. L.).
332. 39:500-1 (April, 1877) *Is That All** (G. P. L.).
333. 39:500-1 (April, 1877) Julia Fletcher, *Kismet** (G. P. L.).
334. 39:501 (April, 1877) *The Great Match and Other Matches** (G. P. L.).
335. 39:506-8 (April, 1877) Berthold Auerbach, *Nach dreissig Jahren** (T. S. P.).
336. 39:632-3 (May, 1877) Philip Gilbert Hamerton, *Wenderholme; a story of Lancashire and Yorkshire** (H. W. P.).
337. 39:637-40 (May, 1877) Honoré de Balzac, *Correspondence** (T. S. P.).
338. 39:752-3 (June, 1877) *Charles Kingsley: his Letters and Memories of his Life** (W. D. H.).
339. 39:759 (June, 1877) Sarah Orne Jewett, *Deephaven** (W. D. H.).
340. 39:761-3 (June, 1877) Émile Zola, *L'Assommoir** (T. S. P.).
341. 40:108-9 (July, 1877) Henry James, *The American** (G. P. L.).
342. 40:109 (July, 1877) *A Modern Mephistopheles** (G. P. L.).
343. 40:109-10 (July, 1877) *Afterglow** (W. D. H.).
344. 40:110-11 (July, 1877) William Black, *Madcap Violet** (T. S. P.).
345. 40:111 (July, 1877) Alphonse Daudet, *Sidonie*, translation* (T. S. P.).
346. 40:111 (July, 1877) Gail Hamilton, *First Love is Best** (G. P. L.).

Criticism of Fiction

347. 40:122-4 (July, 1877) Ivan Turgénieff, *Terres Vièrges*, French translation* (T. S. P.).
348. 40:227-33 (August, 1877) E. P. Whipple, "The Shadow on Dickens's Life."
349. 40:242-3 (August, 1877) Julian Hawthorne, *Garth** (G. P. L.).
350. 40:290-5 (September, 1877) Eugene Benson, "A Study of De Stendhal."
351. 40:327-33 (September, 1877) E. P. Whipple, "Dickens's *Great Expectations*."
352. 40:381-2 (September, 1877) Henry Gréville, *Les Koumiassine** (T. S. P.)
353. 40:382 (September, 1877) Henry Gréville, *La Princesse Oghérof** (T. S. P.).
354. 40:382-3 (September, 1877) Gustave Flaubert, *Trois Contes** (T. S. P.).
355. 40:383 (September, 1877) Gustave Haller, *Le Bleuet** (T. S. P.).
356. 40:383-4 (September, 1877) Friedrich Spielhagen, *Sturmflut** (T. S. P.).
357. 40:507-8 (October, 1877) Charles Reade, *A Woman Hater*.*
358. 40:508-9 (October, 1877) *Nimport** (H. E. S.).
359. 40:508-9 (October, 1877) Anthony Trollope, *An American Senator.**
360. 40:630-1 (November, 1877) F. H. Burnett, *That Lass o' Lowrie's** (G. P. L.).
361. 40:631-2 (November, 1877) John Esten Cooke, *Canolles** (J. M. Bugbee).
362. 40:634 (November, 1877) Victor Cherbuliez, *Samuel Brohl et Cie** (T. S. P.).
363. 40:635-6 (November, 1877) Wilhelm Jensen, *Fluth und Ebbe** (T. S. P.).
364. 40:763-4 (December, 1877) C. D. Warner, *Being a Boy** (W. D. H.).
365. 40:764 (December, 1877) E. Werner, *Vineta, the Phantom City*, translation* (T. S. P.).
366. 41:141 (January, 1878) T. B. Aldrich, *The Queen of Sheba** (W. D. H.).

367. 41:142 (January, 1878) F. H. Burnett, *Surly Tim and Other Stories.**
368. 41:180-8 (February, 1878) Elie Reclus, "Edmond and Jules Goncourt."
369. 41:404 (March, 1878) J. L. Crane, *The Two Circuits: a Story of Illinois Life** (T. S. P.).
370. 41:406 (March, 1878) Ausburn Towner, *Chedayne of Kotono: a Story of the Early Days of the Republic** (T. S. P.).
371. 41:486-9 (April, 1878) E. S. Phelps, *The Story of Avis.** (H. W. P.).
372. 41:489-91 (April, 1878) William Black, *Green Pastures and Piccadilly.** (H. W. P.).
373. 41:492 (April, 1878) Richard D. Blackmore, *Erema; or, My Father's Sin.** (H. W. P.).
374. 41:491 (April, 1878) *Marjorie Bruce's Lovers** (H. W. P.).
375. 41:492-3 (April, 1878) Mrs. Leith Adams, *Winstowe** (H. W. P.).
376. 41:493 (April, 1878) *A Modern Minister** (H. W. P.).
377. 41:493-4 (April, 1878) *The Wolf at the Door** (H. W. P.).
378. 41:494 (April, 1878) [Blanche Willis Howard], *One Summer** (H. W. P.).
379. 41:551 (April, 1878) W. W. Follett Synge, *Olivia Raleigh.**
380. 41:669 (May, 1878) Charles Dickens, *Works*, illustrated edition* (W. D. H.).
381. 42:118-19 (July, 1878) Henry James, *French Poets and Novelists** (W. D. H.).
382. 42:188-92 (August, 1878) W. H. Mallock, *The New Republic.** (H. W. P.).
383. 42:192 (August, 1878) *The Sarcasm of Destiny** (H. W. P.).
384. 42:193-5 (August, 1878) Julia Fletcher, *Kismet* Mirage** (H. W. P.).
385. 42:195-7 (August, 1878) Hesba Stretton, *Through a Needle's Eye** (H. W. P.).
386. 42:197 (August, 1878) Mrs. Charles, *Lapsed but not Lost** (H. W. P.)
387. 42:198 (August, 1878) Henry Gréville, *Dosia** (H. W. P.).
388. 42:296-8 (September, 1878) Alexander Gontcharoff, *Oblomoff** (T. S. P.).

Criticism of Fiction

389. 42:298-9 (September, 1878) Alphonse Daudet, *Le Nabab** (T. S. P.).
390. 42:299-301 (September, 1878) Honoré de Balzac, *Les Petits Bourgeois** (T. S. P.).
391. 42:301-3 (September, 1878) Henry Gréville, *Dosia** *Sonia** *Nouvelles Russes** (T. S. P.).
392. 42:303 (September, 1878) Gustave Haller, *Vertu** (T. S. P.)
393. 42:303-4 (September, 1878) Émile Zola, *Une Page d'Amour** (T. S. P.)
394. 42:430 (October, 1878) L. W. Champney, *Bourbon Lilies** (H. W. P.).
395. 42:430 (October, 1878) *Seola** (H. W. P.).
396. 42:431 (October, 1878) *Gemini** (H. W. P.).
397. 42:431 (October, 1878) Harriet Beecher Stowe, *Poganuc People** (H. W. P.).
398. 42:432 (October, 1878) Bret Harte, *The Story of a Mine** (H. W. P.).
399. 42:432-4 (October, 1878) William M. Baker, *A Year Worth Living** (H. W. P.).
400. 42:434 (October, 1878) Frederic Whittaker, *The Cadet Button** (H. W. P.).
401. 42:434-5 (October, 1878) *Justine's Lovers** (H. W. P.).
402. 42:435-6 (October, 1878) Alice Perry, *Esther Pennefather** (H. W. P.)
403. 42:697 (December, 1878) [Edward Bellamy], *Six to One** (H. W. P.)
404. 42:697-8 (December, 1878) *Brief Honors** (H. W. P.).
405. 42:698 (December, 1878) [Anne Trumbull Slosson], *The China Hunters Club** (H. W. P.).
406. 42:698-9 (December, 1878) E. P. Tenney, *Agamenticus** (H. W. P.).
407. 42:699 (December, 1878) M. J. Savage, *Bluffton** (H. W. P.).
408. 42:699-700 (December, 1878) John Habberton, *The Crew of the Sam Weller** (H. W. P.).
409. 42:700 (December, 1878) Alma Calder, *Miriam's Heritage** (H. W. P.).
410. 42:700 (December, 1878) *Mag** (H. W. P.).

411. 42:700-1 (December, 1878) [H. H. Jackson], *Saxe Holm Stories** (H. W. P.).
412. 42:701 (December, 1878) Bret Harte, *Drift from Two Shores** (H. W. P.).
413. 42:701 (December, 1878) James Payn, *Less Black than We're Painted** (H. W. P.).
414. 42:702 (December, 1878) J. C. Lockhart, *Mine is Thine** (H. W. P.).
415. 42:702 (December, 1878) Henry Gréville, *Gabrielle** (H. W. P.).
416. 42:702 (December, 1878) E. Juncker, *Margarethe*, translation* (H. W. P.).
417. 42:702 (December, 1878) Wilhelm Bergsoe, *Pillone*, translation* (H. W. P.).
418. 42:702 (December, 1878) Leo Tolstoy, *The Cossacks** (H. W. P.).
419. 42:703-5 (December, 1878) *Colonel Dunwoddie, Millionaire** (H. W. P.).
420. 42:705-6 (December, 1878) Sherwood Bonner, *Like Unto Like** (H. W. P.).
421. 43:167-9 (February, 1879) Henry James, *The Europeans** (H. W. P.).
422. 43:169-70 (February, 1879) M. L. Scudder, Jr., *Almost an Englishman** (H. W. P.).
423. 43:170 (February, 1879) Clara Frances Morse, *Blush Roses** (H. W. P.)
424. 43:170-2 (February, 1879) *Molly Bawn** (H. W. P.).
425. 43:172 (February, 1879) Mary A. Denison, *Old Slip Warehouse** (H. W. P.).
426. 43:172-3 (February, 1879) James Kent, *Sibyl Spencer** (H. W. P.).
427. 43:407-8 (March, 1879) Harriet Beecher Stowe, *Uncle Tom's Cabin*, new edition.*
428. 43:500-2 (April, 1879) Thomas Hardy, *The Return of the Native** (H. W. P.).
429. 43:502-4 (April, 1879) William Black, *Macleod of Dare** (H. W. P.).

430. 43:504 (April, 1879) M. A. Tincker, *Signor Monaldini's Niece** (H. W. P.).
431. 43:504-5 (April, 1879) Edward Eggleston, *Roxy** (H. W. P.).
432. 43:548-9 (April, 1879) Victor Cherbuliez, *L'Idée de Jean Téterol** (T. S. P.).
433. 43:548 (April, 1879) Louis Ulbach, *Simple Amour** (T. S. P.).
434. 43:549 (April, 1879) Marie Uchard, *L'Étoile de Jean** (T. S. P.).
435. 43:549 (April, 1879) Henry Gréville, *Marier sa Fille** (T. S. P.).
436. 43:549-50 (April, 1879) Paul Heyse, *Das Ding an sich und Andere** (T. S. P.).
437. 43:686-8 (May, 1879) Octave Feuillet, *Le Journal d'une Femme** (T. S. P.).
438. 43:650-6 (May, 1879) Clara Barnes Martin, "Emile Zola as a Critic."
439. 43:751 (June, 1879) Trebor, *As it May Happen** (H. W. P.).
440. 43:752 (June, 1879) William M. Baker, *The Virginians in Texas** (H. W. P.).
441. 43:752 (June, 1879) Charles De Kay, *The Bohemians** (H. W. P.).
442. 43:753 (June, 1879) E. L. Bynner, *Tritons** (H. W. P.).
443. 43:753 (June, 1879) Henry Gréville, *Philomène's Marriage** (H. W. P.).
444. 43:753-4 (June, 1879) Mrs. A. E. Porter, *Cousin Polly's Gold Mine** (H. W. P.).
445. 43:755-7 (June, 1879) Samuel Adams Drake, *Captain Nelson** (H. W. P.).
446. 43:757 (June, 1879) Robert Lowell, *Stories from an Old Dutch Town** (H. W. P.).
447. 43:758 (June, 1879) Martha Finley, *Signing the Contract and What it Cost** (H. W. P.).
448. 43:758-9 (June, 1879) Henry James, *An International Episode** (H. W. P.).
449. 44:264-5 (August, 1879) W. H. Bishop, *Detmold; a Romance** (W. D. H.).

450. 44:267-8 (August, 1879) Anthony Trollope, *Thackeray** (W. D. H.).
451. 44:361-4 (September, 1879) F. Hassaurek, *The Secret of the Andes** (H. W. P.).
452. 44:364 (September, 1879) *The Puritan and The Quaker** (H. W. P.).
453. 44:364-5 (September, 1879) Hjalmar Hjorth Boyesen, *Falconberg** (H. W. P.).
454. 44:366 (September, 1879) Jessie Fothergill, *First Violin** (H. W. P.)
455. 44:366 (September, 1879) *Airy Fairy Lillian** (H. W. P.)
456. 44:367 (September, 1879) F. H. Burnett, *Kathleen Mavourneen* Theo* Pretty Polly Pemberton** (H. W. P.).
457. 44:368 (September, 1879) Henry Gréville, *Markof, the Russian Violinist** (H. W. P.).
458. 44:369 (September, 1879) *The Colonel's Opera Cloak** (H. W. P.).
459. 44:383-93 (September, 1879) W. H. Bishop, "Story Paper Literature."
460. 44:685 (November, 1879) Paul Heusy, *Un Coin de la Vie de Misère** (T. S. P.).
461. 44:686 (November, 1879) A. Theuriet, *La Maison des Deux Barbeaux** (T. S. P.).
462. 44:686-7 (November, 1879) Berthold Auerbach, *Landolin von Reutershöfen** (T. S. P.).
463. 44:761-70 (December, 1879) Clara Barnes Martin, "The Greatest Novelist's Work for Freedom" [Turgénieff].
464. 44:808-9 (December, 1879) Émile Zola, *Mes Haines** (T. S. P.).
465. 44:809-10 (December, 1879) Edmond de Goncourt, *Les Frères Zemganno.**
466. 45:44-5 (January, 1880) George Washington Cable, *Old Creole Days** (H. W. P.).
467. 45:46-7 (January, 1880) Jean Ingelow, *Sarah de Berenger** (H. W. P.).
468. 45:48 (January, 1880) *A Man's a Man for a' That** (H. W. P.).

469. 45:48-9 (January, 1880) John Boyle O'Reilly, *Moondyne** (H. W. P.).
470. 45:49-50 (January, 1880) S. B. Elliott, *The Felmeres** (H. W. P.).
471. 45:50-1 (January, 1880) E. S. Phelps, *Sealed Orders** (H. W. P.).
472. 45:51-2 (January, 1880) B. M. Butt, *Delicia** (H. W. P.).
473. 45:52-3 (January, 1880) Mary A. Sprague, *An Earnest Trifler** (H. W. P.).
474. 45:117-19 (January, 1880) Alphonse Daudet, *Les Rois en Exil** (H. W. P.).
475. 45:119 (January, 1880) Luigi Gualdo, *Un Mariage Excentrique.**
476. 45:280-2 (February, 1880) Charles Dickens, *Letters** (W. D. H.).
477. 45:282-5 (February, 1880) Henry James, *Hawthorne** (W. D. H.).
478. 45:394 (March, 1880) E. Bergerat, *Théophile Gautier** (T. S. P.).
479. 45:396-408 (March, 1880) C. D. Warner, "Washington Irving."
480. 45:450-64 (April, 1880) H. W. Preston, *A Woman of Genius* [Madame Henrietta Paalzow].
481. 45:566-70 (April, 1880) Berthold Auerbach, *Unterwegs** Der Forstmeister** (T. S. P.).
482. 45:570 (April, 1880) Wilhelmine von Hillern, *Und sie kommt doch!** (T. S. P.).
483. 45:678-9 (May, 1880) Jessie Fothergill, *Probation** (H. E. S.).
484. 45:679 (May, 1880) Amanda M. Douglas, *Hope Mills** (H. E. S.).
485. 45:680-1 (May, 1880) J. W. De Forest, *Irene, the Missionary** (H. E. S.).
486. 45:681 (May, 1880) Dinah M. Craik, *Young Mrs. Jardine** (H. E. S.).
487. 45:682-3 (May, 1880) Albion W. Tourgeé, *Figs and Thistles** (H. E. S.).
488. 45:684 (May, 1880) Andre Theuriet, *Angèle's Fortune** (H. E. S.).

489. 45:685-6 (May, 1880) Sarah Orne Jewett, *Old Friends and New** (H. E. S.).
490. 45:686-8 (May, 1880) Mark Twain, *A Tramp Abroad** (W. D. H.).
491. 45:693-9 (May, 1880) Émile Zola, *Nana** (T. S. P.).
492. 46:121-2 (July, 1880) Gilbert A. Pierce, *Zachariah the Congressman** (T. S. P.).
493. 46:122 (July, 1880) *Her Ladyship** (T. S. P.).
494. 46:122 (July, 1880) D. A. Moore, *How She Won Him** (T. S. P.).
495. 46:122-3 (July, 1880) W. O. Stoddard, *The Heart of It** (T. S. P.).
496. 46:123 (July, 1880) Anne Keary, *A Doubting Heart** (T. S. P.).
497. 46:124 (July, 1880) W. M. F. Round, *Hal, the Story of a Clodhopper** (T. S. P.).
498. 46:124 (July, 1880) Arthur Griffiths, *A Wayward Woman** (T. S. P.)
499. 46:124-5 (July, 1880) Constance Fenimore Woolson, *Rodman the Keeper** (T. S. P.)
500. 46:125 (July, 1880) Théophile Gautier, *Captain Fracasse** (T. S. P.).
501. 46:125-6 (July, 1880) Henry James, *Confidence** (T. S. P.).
502. 46:123 (July, 1880) *Mademoiselle de Mersac** (T. S. P.).
503. 46:313-19 (September, 1880) T. S. Perry, "Sir Walter Scott."
504. 46:412-13 (September, 1880) Mrs. A. D. Whitney, *Odd or Even?** (H. E. S.).
505. 46:414 (September, 1880) Sylvester Judd, *Richard Edney and the Governor's Family** (H. E. S.).
506. 46:414-15 (September, 1880) F. H. Burnett, *Louisiana** (H. E. S.).
507. 46:415-16 (September, 1880) Edgar Fawcett, *A Hopeless Case** (H. E. S.).
508. 46:416-17 (September, 1880) Jane G. Austin, *Mrs. Beauchamp Brown** (H. E. S.).
509. 46:417 (September, 1880) Frank Stockton, *Rudder Grange**
510. 46:417-18 (September, 1880) Helen Campbell, *Unto the Third and Fourth Generations** (H. E. S.).

511. 46:419 (September, 1880) L. Clarke Davis, *A Stranded Ship** (H. E. S.).
512. 46:419 (September, 1880) *A Foreign Marriage** (H. E. S.).
513. 46:419-20 (September, 1880) Annette Lucille Noble, *Uncle Jack's Executor** (H. E. S.).
514. 46:421 (September, 1880) Carroll Winchester, *From Madge to Margaret** (H. E. S.).
515. 46:421-2 (September, 1880) Henry Adams, *Democracy** (H. E. S.).
516. 46:422-4 (September, 1880) Albion Tourgée, *A Fool's Errand** (H. E. S.).
517. 46:695-8 (November, 1880) W. D. Howells, "Mr. Aldrich's Fiction."
518. 46:767-77 (December, 1880) H. W. Preston, "The Later Writings of Mr. Mallock."
519. 46:824-6 (December, 1880) Edward Bellamy, *Dr. Heidenhoff's Process** (H. E. S.).
520. 46:826-7 (December, 1880) Richard D. Blackmore, *Mary Anerly** (H. E. S.).
521. 46:827-8 (December, 1880) John Esten Cooke, *The Virginia Bohemians** (H. E. S.).
522. 46:828 (December, 1880) Richard Meade Bache, *Under the Palmetto** (H. E. S.).
523. 46:828 (December, 1880) Robert E. Ballard, *Myrtle Lawn** (H. E. S.).
524. 46:828 (December, 1880) Mrs. Elizabeth Van Loon, *Mystery of Allanwold** (H. E. S.).
525. 46:829-31 (December, 1880) George Washington Cable, *The Grandissimes** (H. E. S.).
526. 46:831-2 (December, 1880) *A Famous Victory** (H. E. S.).
527. 46:832 (December, 1880) Mary Laffan, *Christy Carew** (H. E. S.).
528. 46:832-3 (December, 1880) L. B. Walford, *Troublesome Daughter** (H. E. S.).
529. 46:833-4 (December, 1880) Jessie Fothergill, *The Wellfields** (H. E. S.).
530. 46:834 (December, 1880) *Beauty's Daughter** (H. E. S.).

531. 46:834 (December, 1880) William Black, *White Wings** (H. E. S.).
532. 46:835 (December, 1880) Anthony Trollope, *The Duke's Children** (H. E. S.).
533. 46:836 (December, 1880) E. M. H. *The Octagon Club** (H. E. S.).
534. 46:836 (December, 1880) *Tit for Tat** (H. E. S.).
535. 46:836 (December, 1880) *Clara Lanza** (H. E. S.).
536. 46:837 (December, 1880) George Bailey, *Oliver Oldboy** (H. E. S.).
537. 46:837-8 (December, 1880) *Salvage** (H. E. S.).
538. 47:116-19 (January, 1881) Émile Zola, *Le Roman Expérimental** (T. S. P.).
539. 47:120 (January, 1881) Albion W. Tourgée, *Bricks Without Straw** (H. E. S.).
540. 47:121 (January, 1881) *A Year of Wreck** (H. E. S.).
541. 47:121 (January, 1881) *How I Found It North and South** (H. E. S.).
542. 47:281-3 (February, 1881) Horace E. Scudder, *Stories and Romances** (S. Kirk).
543. 47:281-3 (February, 1881) P. Deming, *Adirondack Stories** (S. Kirk).
544. 47:284 (February, 1881) S. Weir Mitchell, *Hepzibah Guiness** *Thee and You** *A Draft on the Bank of Spain** (S. Kirk).
545. 47:284 (February, 1881) Nora Perry, *Tragedy of the Unexpected** (S. Kirk).
546. 47:575-7 (April, 1881) Gustave Freytag, *Aus einer kleinen Stadt** (T. S. P.).
547. 47:575-7 (April, 1881) Berthold Auerbach, *Brigitta** (T. S. P.).
548. 47:707-9 (May, 1881) George Fleming, *The Head of Medusa** (H. E. S.).
549. 47:709-10 (May, 1881) Henry James, *Washington Square** (H. E. S.).
550. 47:710-11 (May, 1881) Lew Wallace, *Ben Hur** (H. E. S.).
551. 47:712-13 (May, 1881) Thomas Hardy, *The Trumpet Major** (H. E. S.).

Criticism of Fiction

552. 47:713 (May, 1881) Frances Mary Peard, *Mother Molly** (H. E. S.).
553. 47:713 (May, 1881) Harry W. French, *Ego** (H. E. S.).
554. 47:713-4 (May, 1881) *My Marriage** (H. E. S.).
555. 47:714 (May, 1881) Leonard Kip, *Nestlenook** (H. E. S.).
556. 47:714-15 (May, 1881) Wilson J. Vance, *Princes' Favors** (H. E. S.).
557. 47:715-16 (May, 1881) Benjamin Disraeli, *Endymion** (H. E. S.).
558. 47:860-1 (June, 1881) M. A. Tincker, *By the Tiber** (H. E. S.).
559. 47:861 (June, 1881) *The Tsar's Widow** (H. E. S.).
560. 47:861 (June, 1881) Frances Campbell Sparhawk, *A Lazy Man's Work** (H. E. S.).
561. 47:861-2 (June, 1881) F. H. Burnett, *A Fair Barbarian** (H. E. S.).
562. 47:862 (June, 1881) *A Nameless Nobleman** (H. E. S.).
563. 48:402-5 (September, 1881) William Dean Howells, *A Fearful Responsibility and Other Stories** (T. B. Aldrich).
564. 48:560-1 (October, 1881) W. H. Mallock, *A Romance of the Nineteenth Century** (M. L. Henry).
565. 48:561-4 (October, 1881) Edgar Fawcett, *A Gentleman of Leisure**
566. 48:564-6 (October, 1881) *Baby Rue.**
567. 48:566-8 (October, 1881) E. S. Phelps, *Friends; a Duet.**
568. 48:568-9 (October, 1881) M. L. Gagneur, *A Nihilist Princess*, translation.*
569. 48:569-70 (October, 1881) Björnstjerne Björnson, *Synnöve Solbakken** (H. E. S.).
570. 48:843-5 (December, 1881) Mark Twain, *The Prince and the Pauper**
571. 49:126-8 (January, 1882) Henry James, *The Portrait of a Lady** (H. E. S.).
572. 49:128-30 (January, 1882) William Dean Howells, *Dr. Breen's Practice** (H. E. S.).
573. 49:846-51 (June, 1882) Henry James, "Alphonse Daudet."
574. 50:111-13 (July, 1882) Constance Fenimore Woolson, *Anne** (H. E. S.).

575. 50:113-15 (July, 1882) G. P. Lathrop, *In the Distance* An Echo of Passion** (H. E. S.).
576. 50:271-4 (August, 1882) Theodore Child, "A Note on Flaubert."
577. 50:264-8 (August, 1882) Bret Harte, *Sketches and Stories** (H. E. S.).
578. 50:709-13 (November, 1882) William Dean Howells, *A Modern Instance** (H. E. S.).
579. 50:839-44 (December, 1882) Lydia Maria Child, *Letters** (H. E. S.).
580. 51:127-31 (January, 1883) Horace E. Scudder, "Björnstjerne Björnson's Stories."
581. 51:243-8 (February, 1883) Maria Louise Henry, "The Morality of Thackeray and George Eliot."
582. 51:266-70 (February, 1883) George Sand, *Correspondence.**
583. 51:363-75 (March, 1883) G. P. Lathrop, "The Hawthorne Manuscripts."
584. 51:408-10 (March, 1883) Francis Marion Crawford, *Mr. Isaacs** (G. P. L.).
585. 51:411 (March, 1883) Margaret Lee, *Divorce** (G. P. L.).
586. 51:412-13 (March, 1883) Charles M. Clay, *A Modern Hagar** (G. P. L.).
587. 51:413 (March, 1883) Adolf Moses, *Luser the Watchmaker** (G. P. L.).
588. 51:413-16 (March, 1883) H. E. Scudder, "Two Women of Letters" [Maria Edgeworth, Mary Russell Mitford].
589. 51:464-74 (April, 1883) Charles Dudley Warner, "Modern Fiction."
590. 51:540-2 (April, 1883) T. R. Lounsbury, *James Fenimore Cooper** (H. E. S.).
591. 51:704-6 (May, 1883) Julian Hawthorne, *Dust** (H. E. S.).
592. 51:706-7 (May, 1883) Henry James, *The Siege of London** (H. E. S.).
593. 51:707-9 (May, 1883) Arthur S. Hardy, *But Yet a Woman** (H. E. S.).
594. 52:118-19 (July, 1883) Mary Hallock Foote, *The Led Horse Claim** (H. E. S.).

Criticism of Fiction

595. 52:119-20 (July, 1883) Constance Fenimore Woolson, *For the Major** (H. E. S.).
596. 52:121-3 (July, 1883) F. H. Burnett, *Through One Administration** (H. E. S.).
597. 52:135-7 (July, 1883) Austin Dobson, *Fielding** (H. E. S.).
598. 52:388-93 (September, 1883) Prosper Mériemé, *Letters** (M. L. Henry).
599. 52:406-8 (September, 1883) Samuel Clemens, *Life on the Mississippi** (G. P. L.).
600. 52:704-5 (November, 1883) William Dean Howells, *A Woman's Reason** (H. E. S.).
601. 52:705-6 (November, 1883) Bret Harte, *In the Carquinez Woods** (H. E. S.).
602. 53:42-55 (January, 1884) Henry James, "Ivan Turgénieff."
603. 53:136-8 (January, 1884) Mrs. Oliphant, *A Little Pilgrim** (H. E. S.).
604. 53:138-41 (January, 1884) E. S. Phelps, *Beyond the Gates** (H. E. S.).
605. 53:141-3 (January, 1884) William M. Baker, *A Blessed Ghost** (H. E. S.).
606. 53:267-71 (February, 1884) Anthony Trollope, *An Autobiography** (H. E. S.).
607. 53:277-9 (February, 1884) Francis Marion Crawford, *To Leeward** (H. E. S.).
608. 53:707-8 (May, 1884) George Fleming, *Vestigia** (G. P. L.).
609. 53:708-9 (May, 1884) [John Hay], *The Bread-Winners** (G. P. L.).
610. 53:710-11 (May, 1884) Edgar Fawcett, *An Ambitious Woman** (G. P. L.).
611. 53:711-12 (May, 1884) Julian Hawthorne, *Beatrix Randolph** (G. P. L.).
612. 53:712-13 (May, 1884) Sarah Orne Jewett, *The Mate of the Daylight** (G. P. L.).
613. 53:717-21 (May, 1884) Owen Meredith, *Life, Letters, and Literary Remains of Edward Bulwer, Lord Lytton*, Vol. II.*
614. 53:850-3 (June, 1884) Edgar E. Saltus, *Balzac** (G. P. L.).
615. 53:857-9 (June, 1884) Paul Bourget, *Essais de Psychologie Contemporaine** (T. Child).

616. 54:131-3 (July, 1884) Charles Egbert Craddock, *In the Tennessee Mountains** (G. P. L.).
617. 54:413-16 (September, 1884) Edward Bellamy, *Miss Ludington's Sister** (H. E. S.).
618. 54:417-18 (September, 1884) J. S. of Dale [Frederick J. Stimson], *The Crime of Henry Vane** (H. E. S.).
619. 54:418-20 (September, 1884) Sarah Orne Jewett, *A Country Doctor** (H. E. S.).
620. 54:420-1 (September, 1884) *Phoebe** (H. E. S.).
621. 54:421-2 (September, 1884) Francis Marion Crawford, *A Roman Singer** (H. E. S.).
622. 54:759-69 (December, 1884) Frank T. Marzials, "Francois Coppée."
623. 54:796-805 (December, 1884) G. P. Lathrop, "Combination Novels."
624. 55:121-3 (January, 1885) George Washington Cable, *Dr. Sevier** (H. E. S.).
625. 55:123 (January, 1885) S. Weir Mitchell, *In War Time** (H. E. S.).
626. 55:123-5 (January, 1885) Charles Egbert Craddock, *Where the Battle Was Fought** (H. E. S.).
627. 55:125-7 (January, 1885) E. W. Howe, *The Story of a Country Town** (H. E. S.).
628. 55:127-30 (January, 1885) Helen Hunt Jackson, *Ramona** (H. E. S.).
629. 55:130-2 (January, 1885) Francis Marion Crawford, *An American Politician**
630. 55:259-65 (February, 1885) Julian Hawthorne, *Nathaniel Hawthorne and his Wife** (T. W. H.).
631. 55:361-71 (March, 1885) Clara Barnes Martin, "The Mother of Turgénieff."
632. 55:668-78 (May, 1885) Henry James, "George Eliot's Life."
633. 55:733-44 (June, 1885) H. W. Preston, "Mrs. Oliphant."
634. 55:846-8 (June, 1885) Henry F. Keenan, *Trajan** (H. E. S.).
635. 55:848 (June, 1885) Harford Fleming, *A Carpet Knight** (H. E. S.).
636. 55:848-9 (June, 1885) Marion Reeves and Emily Read, *Pilot Fortune** (H. E. S.).

Criticism of Fiction

637. 55:849-51 (June, 1885) Barrett Wendell, *The Duchess Emilia** (H. E. S.).
638. 56:85-7 (July, 1885) E. E. Hale, "Daniel Defoe and Thomas Shepard."
639. 56:230-42 (August, 1885) H. W. Preston, "Miss Ingelow and Mrs. Walford."
640. 56:273-7 (August, 1885) Walter Pater, *Marius the Epicurean** (H. E. S.).
641. 56:554-6 (October, 1885) William Dean Howells, *The Rise of Silas Lapham** (H. E. S.).
642. 56:556-8 (October, 1885) Charles Egbert Craddock, *The Prophet of the Great Smoky Mountains** (H. E. S.).
643. 56:558-60 (October, 1885) Blanche Willis Howard, *Aulnay Tower** (H. E. S.).
644. 56:560-1 (October, 1885) Sarah Orne Jewett, *A Marsh Island** (H. E. S.).
645. 56:561-2 (October, 1885) Francis Marion Crawford, *Zoroaster** (H. E. S.).
646. 57:258-9 (February, 1886) Arlo Bates, *A Wheel of Fire** (H. E. S.).
647. 57:260-1 (February, 1886) Sidney Luska, *As it Was Written** (H. E. S.).
648. 57:261-3 (February, 1886) Brander Matthews, *Last Meeting** (H. E. S.).
649. 57:263-4 (February, 1886) T. R. Sullivan, *Roses of Shadow** (H. E. S.).
650. 57:264-5 (February, 1866) Howard Pyle, *Within the Capes** (H. E. S.).
651. 57:265-6 (February, 1886) George H. Picard, *A Mission Flower** (H. E. S.).
652. 57:266-8 (February, 1886) Frances Courtenay Baylor, *On Both Sides** (H. E. S.).
653. 57:268-9 (February, 1886) Mary Spear Tiernan, *Suzette**
654. 57:269-70 (February, 1886) M. G. McClelland, *Oblivion** (H. E. S.).
655. 57:270-1 (February, 1886) William Waldorf Astor, *Valentino** (H. E. S.).

656. 57:471-85 (April, 1886) Julian Hawthorne, "Problems of *The Scarlet Letter.*"
657. 57:834-50 (June, 1886) George Frederic Parsons, "Honoré de Balzac."
658. 57:850-3 (June, 1886) Henry James, *The Bostonians** (H. E. S.).
659. 57:853-4 (June, 1886) Francis Marion Crawford, *A Tale of a Lonely Parish** (H. E. S.).
660. 57:855-6 (June, 1886) William Dean Howells, *Indian Summer** (H. E. S.).
661. 58:47-58 (July, 1886) H. W. Preston, "Ouida."
662. 58:131-3 (July, 1886) Arthur Sherburne Hardy, *Winds of Destiny** (H. E. S.).
663. 58:133-4 (July, 1886) Frank Stockton, *The Late Mrs. Null** (H. E. S.).
664. 58:267-9 (August, 1886) H. C. Bunner, *The Midge** (H. E. S.).
665. 58:269 (August, 1886) Eleanor Putnam, *Old Salem** (H. E. S.).
666. 58:783-91 (December, 1886) H. W. Preston, "The Church of England Novel."
667. 59:130-2 (January, 1877) Horace E. Scudder, "Stockton's Stories."
668. 59:265-7 (February, 1887) Charles Egbert Craddock, *In the Clouds** (H. E. S.).
669. 59:267-8 (February, 1887) Constance Fenimore Woolson, *East Angels** (H. E. S.).
670. 59:268-9 (February, 1887) M. G. McClelland, *Princess** (H. E. S.).
671. 59:269-71 (February, 1887) Charlotte Dunning, *A Step Aside** (H. E. S.).
672. 59:290-9 (March, 1887) James Breck Perkins, "Théophile Gautier."
673. 60:57-67 (July, 1887) I. F. Hapgood, "Count Tolstoi and the Public Censor."
674. 60:145-57 (August, 1887) E. E. House, "Personal Characteristics of Charles Reade."

675. 60:199-213 (August, 1887) H. W. Preston, "The Spell of the Russian Writers."
676. 60:413-14 (August, 1887) Francis Marion Crawford, *Saracinesca** (H. E. S.).
677. 60:414-15 (August, 1887) H. C. Bunner, *The Story of a New York House** (H. E. S.).
678. 60:415-16 (August, 1887) Sidney Luska, *The Yoke of the Thorah** (H. E. S.).
679. 60:417-18 (August, 1887) Frances Courtenay Baylor, *Behind the Blue Ridge**
680. 60:525-39 (October, 1887) E. H. House, "Anecdotes of Charles Reade."
681. 60:705-14 (November, 1887) H. W. Preston, "Girl Novelists of the Time" [Emily Bronte, *Wuthering Heights**; Alma-Tadema, *Love's Martyr**; Olive Schreiner, *The Story of an African Farm**].
682. 60:714 (November, 1887) James Payn, *Heir of the Ages*.*
683. 60:747-55 (December, 1887) Sophia Kirk, "Robert Louis Stevenson."
684. 60:853-5 (December, 1887) *A Collection of Letters of Thackeray, 1847-1855.**
685. 61:178-93 (February, 1888) G. P. Lathrop, "George Meredith."
686. 61:421-3 (March, 1888) T. Child, "The Goncourt Memoirs."
687. 61:710-14 (May, 1888) G. E. Woodberry, "Charles Brockden Brown."
688. 61:771-82 (June, 1888) Theodore Child, "The Literary Career in France."
689. 61:841-3 (June, 1888) George Washington Cable, *Bonaventure** (H. E. S.).
690. 61:843-5 (June, 1888) Ellen Olney Kirk, *Queen Money** (H. E. S.).
691. 61:845-6 (June, 1888) Edward Bellamy, *Looking Backward.* (H. E. S.).
692. 61:846-7 (June, 1888) D. R. McNally, *Irish Wonders** (H. E. S.).
693. 61:847-8 (June, 1888) Francis Marion Crawford, *Marzio's Crucifix.**

694. 62:564-8 (October, 1888) Henry James, *Partial Portraits** (G. E. Woodberry).
695. 62:700-4 (November, 1888) Mrs. Humphry Ward, *Robert Elsmere** (H. E. S.).
696. 62:704-6 (November, 1888) Margaret Deland, *John Ward, Preacher** (H. E. S.).
697. 62:711-15 (November, 1888) Alphonse Daudet, *L'Immortel** (S. Kirk).
698. 63:274-7 (February, 1889) Edward Eggleston, *The Graysons** (H. E. S.).
699. 63:276-80 (February, 1889) Joseph Kirkland, *The McVeys** (H. E. S.).
700. 64:122-4 (July, 1889) Charles Egbert Craddock, *The Despot of Broomsedge Cove** (H. E. S.).
701. 64:125-6 (July, 1889) Arthur S. Hardy, *Passe Rose** (H. E. S.).
702. 64:126-9 (July, 1889) Elizabeth Stoddard, *Temple House* (H. E. S.).
703. 64:129 (July, 1889) Edward Irenaeus Stevenson, *Janus** (H. E. S.).
704. 64:527-36 (October, 1889) Agnes Repplier, "Fiction in the Pulpit."
705. 65:122-3 (January, 1890) Francis Marion Crawford, *Sant' Ilario** (H. E. S.).
706. 65:123-4 (January, 1890) William Waldorf Astor, *Sforza: a Story of Milan** (H. E. S.).
707. 65:124-6 (January, 1890) Mary Hartwell Catherwood, *The Romance of Dollard** (H. E. S.).
708. 65:126-8 (January, 1890) Constance Fenimore Woolson, *Jupiter Lights** (H. E. S.).
709. 65:128 (January, 1890) Robert Lowell, *The New Priest in Conception Bay** (H. E. S.).
710. 65:563-6 (April, 1890) William Dean Howells, *A Hazard of New Fortunes** (H. E. S.).
711. 65:567-9 (April, 1890) C. D. Warner, *A Little Journey in the World** (H. E. S.).
712. 65:721-31 (June, 1890) C. D. Warner, "The Novel and the Common School."

713. 66:131-3 (July, 1890) E. S. Phelps and H. D. Ward, *The Master of the Magicians**
714. 66:276 (August, 1890) Henri Lavedan, *Les Inconsolables* Sire** (Sophia Kirk).
715. 66:276 (August, 1890) Henri Rabusson, *Idylle et Drame de Salon** (Sophia Kirk).
716. 66:276 (August, 1890) Jules Claretie, *Pierille** (Sophia Kirk).
717. 66:276-8 (August, 1890) Victor Cherbuliez, *Une Gaguerre** (Sophia Kirk).
718. 66:278-9 (August, 1890) Eduoard Rod, *Les Trois Coeurs** (Sophia Kirk).
719. 66:419-22 (September, 1890) Henry James, *The Tragic Muse** (H. E. S.).
720. 66:695-8 (November, 1890) Elbridge S. Brooks, *A Son of Issachar** (H. E. S.).
721. 66:698-9 (November, 1890) William F. Cooley, *Emmanuel; the Story of the Messiah** (H. E. S.).
722. 66:699-700 (November, 1890) E. S. Phelps and H. D. Ward, *Come Forth** (H. E. S.).
723. 67:108-21 (January, 1891) Sophia Kirk, "A Novelist of the Jura" [T. Combe].
724. 67:270-3 (February, 1891) Sir Walter Scott, *Journal*, Vol. II* (H. E. S.).
725. 67:393-402 (March, 1891) Agnes Repplier, "Pleasure: a Heresy."
726. 67:414-16 (March, 1891) Anatole France, *Thais** (Sophia Kirk).
727. 67:416-17 (March, 1891) F. Fabre, *Un Illuminé** (Sophia Kirk).
728. 67:845-50 (June, 1891) Annie Trumbull Slosson, *Seven Dreamers** (H. E. S.).
729. 67:845-50 (June, 1891) Mary E. Wilkins, *A New England Nun** (H. E. S.).
730. 67:845-50 (June, 1891) Sarah Orne Jewett, *Strangers and Wayfarers** (H. E. S.).
731. 68:78-87 (July, 1891) Agnes Repplier, "English Railway Fiction."

Register of Reviews and Critical Essays

732. 68:566-9 (October, 1891) William Dean Howells, *Criticism and Fiction** (H. E. S.).
733. 68:596-620 (November, 1891) Isabel F. Hapgood, "Count Tolstoy at Home."
734. 68:695-9 (November, 1891) Gustave Flaubert, *Correspondence** (Sophia Kirk).
735. 68:699 (November, 1891) Charles Buet, *J. Barbey D'Aurevilly** (Sophia Kirk).
736. 68:699-701 (November, 1891) J. Barbey d'Aurevilly, *Littérature Étrangère** (Sophia Kirk).
737. 68:824-38 (December, 1891) Lida von Krockow, "American Character in German Novels."
738. 69:123-8 (January, 1892) Paul Bourget, *Sensations d'Italie** *Nouveaux Pastels** (Sophia Kirk).
739. 69:123-8 (January, 1892) Pierre Loti, *Le Livre de la Pitié et de la Mort** (Sophia Kirk).
740. 69:262-3 (February, 1892) Thomas Nelson Page, *Elsket and Other Stories** (C. T. Copeland).
741. 69:263-4 (February, 1892) Joel Chandler Harris, *Balaam and His Master** (C. T. C.).
742. 69:264-5 (February, 1892) James Lane Allen, *Flute and Violin** (C. T. C.).
743. 69:265 (February, 1892) Octave Thanet, *Otto the Knight** (C. T. C.).
744. 69:266 (February, 1892) Hamlin Garland, *Main Traveled Roads** (C. T. C.).
745. 69:266-8 (February, 1892) Richard Harding Davis, *Gallegher and Other Stories** (C. T. C.).
746. 69:268 (February, 1892) Elizabeth Stuart Phelps, *Fourteen to One** (C. T. C.).
747. 69:268-9 (February, 1892) Rose Terry Cooke, *Huckleberries** (C. T. C.).
748. 69:269 (February, 1892) Thomas A. Janvier, *The Uncle of an Angel** (C. T. C.).
749. 69:269 (February, 1892) H. C. Bunner, *Zadoc Pine** (C. T. C.).
750. 69:269 (February, 1892) Brander Matthews, *With My Friends** (C. T. C.).

Criticism of Fiction

751. 69:270 (February, 1892) Frank Stockton, *The Rudder Grangers Abroad** (C. T. C.).
752. 69:355-63 (March, 1892) F. Blake Crofton, "Thomas Chandler Haliburton."
753. 69:406-7 (March, 1892) Eduoard Rod, *Stendhal** (Sophia Kirk).
754. 69:694-7 (May, 1892) Charles Egbert Craddock, *In the "Stranger People's" Country** (H. E. S.).
755. 69:697-702 (May, 1892) Thomas Hardy, *Tess of the D'Urbervilles** (C. T. C.).
756. 69:702-4 (May, 1892) William Dean Howells, *The Quality of Mercy** (H. E. S.).
757. 69:704-5 (May, 1892) Mrs. Humphry Ward, *The History of David Grieve** (C. T. C.).
758. 69:705-6 (May, 1892) Mary Hartwell Catherwood, *Lady of Fort St. John** (H. E. S.).
759. 69:706-7 (May, 1892) George Du Maurier, *Peter Ibbetson** (C. T. C.).
760. 70:130-33 (July, 1892) Mary Russell Mitford, *Our Village** (C. T. C.).
761. 70:130-33 (July, 1892) Mrs. Gaskell, *Cranford** (C. T. C.).
762. 70:130-33 (July, 1892) Frances Hodgson Burnett, *A Fair Barbarian** (C. T. C.).
763. 70:276-8 (August, 1892) Matilde Serao, *Il paese di Cuccagna.**
764. 70:402-7 (September, 1892) Friedrich Spielhagen, *Finder und Erfinder** (Lida Krockow).
765. 71:410-15 (March, 1893) Paul Heyse, *Merlin** (Lida Krockow).
766. 71:675-82 (May, 1893) Bliss Perry, "Hawthorne at North Adams."
767. 71:836-46 (June, 1893) C. T. Copeland, "Miss Austen and Miss Ferrier."
768. 72:413-14 (September, 1893) Matilde Serao, *All'erta sentinella** *Conquista di Roma.**
769. 72:413-14 (September, 1893) Daniele Cortis, *Antonio Fogazzaro.**

174

770. 72:693-4 (November, 1893) Francis Marion Crawford, *Pietro Ghisleri** (H. E. S.).
771. 72:695 (November, 1893) Gilbert Parker, *Chief Factor** (H. E. S.).
772. 72:695-6 (November, 1893) Henry James, *The Real Thing and Other Tales** (H. E. S.).
773. 72:696-7 (November, 1893) Annie Eliot, *White Birches** (H. E. S.).
774. 72:697 (November, 1893) Mary Hartwell Catherwood, *Old Kaskaskia** (H. E. S.).
775. 72:697 (November, 1893) Mrs. Burton Harrison, *Belhaven Tales** *An Edelweiss of the Sierras** (H. E. S.).
776. 72:698 (November, 1893) Octave Thanet, *Stories of a Western Town** (H. E. S.).
777. 72:698-9 (November, 1893) Margaret Deland, *Mr. Tommy Dove** (H. E. S.).
778. 73:130-3 (January, 1894) Sarah Orne Jewett, *A Native of Winby** *Deephaven** (H. E. S.).
779. 73:405-9 (March, 1894) Sir Walter Scott, *Letters** (W. Everett).
780. 73:555-7 (April, 1894) Henry B. Fuller, *The Cliff Dwellers** (H. E. S.).
781. 73:557 (April, 1894) Grace King, *Balcony Stories** (H. E. S.).
782. 73:557-8 (April, 1894) Mary Hartwell Catherwood, *The White Islander** (H. E. S.).
783. 73:558-9 (April, 1894) Kate Chopin, *Bayou Folk** (H. E. S.).
784. 74:114-19 (July, 1894) M. L. Thompson, "Baroness Tautphoeus."
785. 74:260-7 (August, 1894) Lida Krockow, "Marie Von Ebner Eschenbach."
786. 74:268-71 (August, 1894) G. R. Carpenter, "A Dumas of the Hour" [Stanley Weyman].
787. 74:272-4 (August, 1894) Mrs. Humphry Ward, *Marcella** (H. E. S.).
788. 74:272-4 (August, 1894) Mary E. Wilkins, *Pembroke** (H. E. S.).
789. 74:521-7 (October, 1894) Henry Childs Merwin, "The Philosophy of Sterne."

Criticism of Fiction

790. 74:701-4 (November, 1894) William Dean Howells, *A Traveler from Altruria** (Sophia Kirk).
791. 74:842-4 (December, 1894) C. Verga, *Don Candeloro**
792. 74:842-4 (December, 1894) L. Capuana, *Le Paesane**
793. 75:108-116 (January, 1895) J. T. Trowbridge, "The Author of *Quabbin*" [F. H. Underwood].
794. 75:266-8 (February, 1895) George Meredith, *Lord Ormont and His Aminta** (W. P. Trent).
795. 75:269 (February, 1895) Hall Caine, *The Manxman** (W. P. Trent).
796. 75:270 (February, 1895) George Du Maurier, *Trilby** (W. P. Trent).
797. 75:316-24 (March, 1895) J. T. Trowbridge, "Some Confessions of a Novel Writer."
798. 75:537-46 (April, 1895) C. T. Copeland, "Robert Louis Stevenson."
799. 75:654-8 (May, 1895) H. E. Scudder, "Richard Harding Davis."
800. 75:817-20 (June, 1895) Rowland Robinson, *Danvis Folks** (C. M. Thompson).
801. 75:820-1 (June, 1895) Charles D. Warner, *The Golden House** (H. E. S.).
802. 75:821-3 (June, 1895) George Washington Cable, *John March, Southerner** (H. E. S.).
803. 75:823-4 (June, 1895) Ellen Olney Kirk, *The Story of Lawrence Garthe** (H. W. P.).
804. 75:824-6 (June, 1895) Paul Leicester Ford, *The Honorable Peter Sterling** (H. E. S.).
805. 76:554-5 (October, 1895) Frank Stockton, *Adventures of Captain Horn** (H. E. S.).
806. 76:555-6 (October, 1895) Henry B. Fuller, *With the Procession** (H. E. S.).
807. 76:556 (October, 1895) Mrs. Burton Harrison, *An Errant Wooing** (H. E. S.).
808. 76:556-7 (October, 1895) Mrs. Humphry Ward, *The Story of Bessie Costrell** (H. E. S.).
809. 76:558 (October, 1895) Bliss Perry, *The Plated City** (H. E. S.).

Register of Reviews and Critical Essays

810. 76:558-9 (October, 1895) Alice Brown, *Meadow Grass** (H. E. S.).
811. 76:701-3 (November, 1895) William Dean Howells, *My Literary Passions** (H. E. S.).
812. 76:840-4 (December, 1895) C. M. Thompson, "New Figures in Literature and Art: Hamlin Garland."
813. 77:173-86 (February, 1896) Rose Hawthorne Lathrop, "Some Memories of Hawthorne" [Also 77:373-87 (March, 1896); 77:492-507 (April, 1896); 77:649-660 (May, 1896)].
814. 77:256-64 (February, 1896) Henry D. Sedgwick, Jr., "Don Quixote."
815. 77:264-5 (February, 1896) Owen Wister, *Red Man and White** (H. E. S.).
816. 77:265-6 (February, 1896) Eliza Orne White, *The Coming of Theodora** (C. M. Thompson).
817. 77:266-7 (February, 1896) E. Hopkinson Smith, *A Gentleman Vagabond** (C. M. Thompson).
818. 77:526-34 (April, 1896) Alice Brown, "Latter-Day Cranford."
819. 77:697-702 (May, 1896) Lida Krockow, "Hermann Sudermann."
820. 78:88-96 (July, 1896) George Washington Cable, "The Speculations of a Story-Teller."
821. 78:145-56 (August, 1896) Annie Fields, "Days with Mrs. Stowe."
822. 78:156-68 (August, 1896) Paul Shorey, "Present Conditions of Literary Production."
823. 78:269-70 (August, 1896) Mary E. Wilkins, *Madelon** (H. E. S.).
824. 78:270-2 (August, 1896) Harold Frederic, *The Damnation of Theron Ware** (H. E. S.).
825. 78:272-3 (August, 1896) Frances Hodgson Burnett, *A Lady of Quality** (H. E. S.).
826. 78:275-6 (August, 1896) Gilbert Parker, *The Seats of the Mighty** (H. E. S.).
827. 78:311-21 (September, 1896) C. D. Warner, "The Story of *Uncle Tom's Cabin*."
828. 78:566-7 (October, 1896) W. P. Trent, "On Reading the Fiftieth Volume of Balzac."

177

Criticism of Fiction

829. 78:673-8 (November, 1896) Charles W. Stoddard, "Early Recollections of Bret Harte."
830. 78:841-3 (December, 1896) Mrs. Humphry Ward, *Sir George Tressady** (H. E. S.).
831. 79:104-110 (January, 1897) Edith Baker Brown, "James Lane Allen."
832. 79:443-50 (April, 1897) Charles Miner Thompson, "Mark Twain as an Interpreter of American Character."
833. 79:705-12 (May, 1897) Frances Courtenay Baylor, "A Reminiscence of Charles Reade."
834. 79:705-7 (May, 1897) Sir James Barrie, *Novels, Tales, Sketches** (H. E. S.).
835. 79:707 (May, 1897) Ian MacClaren, *Kate Carnegie** (H. W. P.).
836. 79:708 (May, 1897) Samuel Crockett, *The Gray Man** (S. M. Francis).
837. 79:708-9 (May, 1897) Flora Annie Steel, *On the Face of the Waters** (S. M. Francis).
838. 79:709 (May, 1897) Henryk Sienkiewicz, *Quo Vadis** (H. W. P.).
839. 79:710 (May, 1897) Walter Pater, *Gaston de Latour** (S. M. Francis).
840. 79:712 (May, 1897) Helen Choate Prince, *A Transatlantic Chatelaine.**
841. 80:143-4 (July, 1897) James Lane Allen, *The Choir Invisible** (H. E. S.).
842. 80:424-7 (September, 1897) Harriet W. Preston, "Mrs. Oliphant."
843. 80:427-30 (September, 1897) Leon H. Vincent, "Concerning a Red Waistcoat" [Théophile Gautier].
844. 80.433-41 (October, 1897) James Lane Allen, "Two Principles in Recent American Fiction."
845. 80:508-22 (October, 1897) Henry D. Sedgwick, Jr., "Gabrielle D'Annunzio."
846. 80:721-8 (December, 1897) Paul Leicester Ford, "The American Historical Novel."
847. 80:753 (December, 1897) T. W. Higginson, "Literary London Twenty Years Ago."

848. 80:846-60 (December, 1897) Robert Louis Stevenson, *St. Ives** (L. Vincent).
849. 80:851-3 (December, 1897) George Du Maurier, *The Martian** (H. W. P.).
850. 80:854-5 (December, 1897) S. Weir Mitchell, *Hugh Wynne** (P. L. Ford).
851. 80:855-7 (December, 1897) Rudyard Kipling, *Captains Courageous** (W. B. Parker).
852. 80:857-9 (December, 1897) Mary E. Wilkins, *Jerome** (C. M. Thompson).
853. 80:859 (December, 1897) William Dean Howells, *An Open-Eyed Conspiracy** (H. W. P.).
854. 80:859-60 (December, 1897) Richard Harding Davis, *Soldiers of Fortune** (M. de W. Howe).
855. 81:81-90 (January, 1898) T. W. Higginson, "Literary Paris Twenty Years Ago."
856. 81:139-44 (January, 1898) Hall Caine, *The Christian** (H. D. Sedgwick, Jr.).
857. 81:289-98 (March, 1898) Henry D. Sedgwick, Jr., "English as Against French Literature."
858. 81:567-73 (April, 1898) William Henry Schofield, "Personal Impressions of Björnson and Ibsen."

INDEX*

Adams, Henry, 515; 127
Adams, Mrs. Leith, 375
Aldrich, Thomas Bailey, 116, 227, 250, 366, 517, 563; 49, 105
Alexander, Mrs., 242
Allen, James Lane, 742, 831, 841, 844; 34, 71
Alma-Tadema, Laurence, 681
Ames, Van Meter, quoted, 101
Andersen, Hans Christian, 132, 139, 164, 293; 19, 106-107
Andersen, Rosmus, 330
Arthur, T. S., 27
Astor, William Waldorf, 655, 706; 28, 57
Auerbach, Berthold, 111, 262, 292, 335, 462, 481, 547; 17, 18, 55
Austen, Jane, 61, 767; 31, 34, 49
Austin, Jane G., 508

Bache, Richard Meade, 522
Bailey, George, 536
Baker, William M., 136, 252, 399, 440, 605; 15, 104
Ballard, Robert E., 523
Balzac, Honoré de, 39, 337, 390, 614, 657, 828; 12, 27, 31, 67
Barbey d'Aurevilly, Jules, 735, 736
Barrie, Sir James, 834
Bates, Arlo, 646; 71, 118-19

Baylor, Frances Courtenay, 652, 679, 833
Beach, Joseph Warren, 39
Beecher, Henry Ward, 103; 67
Bellamy, Edward, 519, 617, 691; 91-92
Benedict, Frank Lee, 137, 259, 287
Benson, Eugene, 102, 350; 81
Bergsöe, Wilhelm, 218, 417
Berriedale, 122; 124
Beyle, Marie Henri, 350, 753; 81
Bierce, Ambrose, 99-100
Bishop, W. H., 449, 459; 22-23
Björnson, Björnstjerne, 118, 143, 569, 580, 858; 17, 18, 31, 88, 104, 106
Black, William, 344, 372, 429, 531; 43, 116
Blackmore, Richard D., 373, 520; 130
Blair, Walter, 98
Bonner, Sherwood, 420
Bourget, Paul, 738
Boyesen, Hjalmar Hjorth, 264, 290, 306, 322, 453; 18, 55
Bronte, Emily, 681
Brooks, Elbridge S., 720
Brown, Alice, 810, 818
Brown, Charles Brockden, 687
Brown, Edith Baker, 831

---

* Numbers in bold-face type refer to the Register of Reviews and Critical Articles which begins on page 137.

181

Criticism of Fiction

Bugbee, J. M., **361**
Bulwer-Lytton, Edward, **240, 613**
Bunner, H. C., **664, 677, 749**
Burnett, Frances Hodgson, **360, 367, 456, 506, 561, 596, 762, 825;** 52, 55
Butt, B. M., **472;** 55-56, 106
Bynner, E. L., **442**

Cable, George Washington, **466, 525, 624, 689, 802, 820;** 17, 36, 46, 68, 124
Caine, Hall, **795, 856;** 53
Calder, Alma, **409**
Campbell, Helen, **510;** 75
Capefigue, Jean, **12**
Capuana, L., **792**
Carpenter, G. R., **786**
Castleton, D. R., **271**
Catherwood, Mary H., **707, 758, 774, 782;** 28-29, 58
Cervantes, Saavedra, Miguel de, **814;** 78
Champfleury, *see* Fleury-Husson, Jules
Champney, Lizzie W., **394**
Charles, Mrs. E. R., **85, 386**
Cherbuliez, Victor, **173, 204, 225, 238, 284, 302, 362, 432, 717;** 43, 81-82, 117, 129
Chesebro', Caroline, **157;** 106
Child, Lydia Marie, **579**
Child, Theodore, **576, 615, 686, 688**
Chopin, Kate, **783;** 22
Churton, Henry, **267**
Claretie, Jules, **716**
Clarke, Mary Cowden, **282**
Clay, Charles M., **586**
Clemens, Samuel, **114, 190, 295, 307, 490, 570, 599, 832;** 36, 55, 99
Collins, Wilkie, **91;** 23, 44
Combe, T., **723**

Conyers, S., **58**
Cooke, John Esten, **255, 361**
Cooke, Rose Terry, **747**
Cooley, William F., **721**
Cooper, James Fenimore, **17, 49, 590;** 12, 16, 41
Copeland, Charles T., **740-51, 755, 757, 759-62, 767, 798;** 34, 71, 78, 95
Coppée, Francois, **622**
Cortis, Daniele, **769**
Craddock, Charles Egbert, *see* Murfree, Mary Noailles
Craik, Dinah M., **486**
Cranch, Christopher P., **234;** 37
Crane, J. L., **369;** 21
Crane, Stephen, 99
Craven, Madame Augustus, **300**
Crawford, Francis Marion, **584, 607, 621, 629, 645, 659, 676, 693, 705, 770;** 50, 59-60, 121
Crockett, Samuel, **836**
Crofton, F. Blake, **752**
Cummins, Maria, **33;** 41, 114
Curtis, George W., **44**

Dana, Richard Henry, **113**
Daudet, Alphonse, **313, 314, 345, 389, 474, 573, 697;** 29, 30, 69, 73, 75
Davis, L. Clarke, **511**
Davis, Rebecca Harding, **249;** 17
Davis, Richard Harding, **745, 799, 854;** 54
Day, Lal Behari, **304**
Defoe, Daniel, **638**
De Forest, John W., **15, 96, 172, 180, 226, 251, 272, 299, 485;** 44, 51, 70, 74, 75-76, 104-105
De Kay, Charles, **441**
Deland, Margaret, **696, 777**
De Mille, James, **130, 191, 206**

182

Index

Deming, P., 543
Denison, Mary A., 425
Deslys, Charles, 317
Dickens, Charles, 43, 45, 53, 95, 108, 126, 135, 138, 155, 156, 158, 162, 167, 176, 210, 244, 309, 319, 324, 348, 351, 380, 476; 71, 96, 115, 122, 128
Dickinson, Anna E., 109
Disraeli, Benjamin, 127, 229, 557; 69, 108
Dodge, L. P., 255, 303
Dodge, Mary A., 65, 84, 346
Dodge, Mary Mapes, 315
Douglas, Amanda M., 484; 75
Drake, Samuel Adams, 445
Droz, Gustave, 159, 200, 283, 296; 29, 30, 45, 66, 110
Du Maurier, George, 759, 796, 849
Dunning, Charlotte, 671

Eastman, Max, 95
Edgeworth, Maria, 81, 588; 31
Edwards, Annie, 182
Eggleston, Edward, 179, 203, 247, 431, 698; 19, 20, 31, 55
Eichendorff, Joseph von, 90
Eliot, Annie, 773
Eliot, George, 7, 18, 32, 92, 215, 320, 581, 632; 11, 14, 28, 29, 31, 41-42, 44-45, 48, 49, 54-55, 65, 68, 92, 117
Elliott, S. B., 470
Emerson, Ralph Waldo, 96, 135
Erckmann-Chatrian, 187; 18
Eschenbach, Marie von Ebner, 785
Everett, W., 779

Fabre, F., 727
Farjeon, B. L., 280
Farrar, Mrs. John, 81
Fawcett, Edgar, 507, 565, 610

Ferrier, Susan, 767
Feuillet, Octave, 193, 437
Feydeau, Ernest, 25
Field, Kate, 73
Fielding, Henry, 597; 48-49
Fields, Annie, 821
Fields, James T., 126, 147, 149, 151, 152, 154, 155, 156, 158, 162, 167, 168, 169
Finley, Martha, 447
Flagg, William, 198; 15
Flaubert, Gustave, 257, 354, 576, 734; 12, 27, 81
Fleming, George, 548, 608
Fleming, Harford, 635
Fletcher, Julia, 333, 384
Fleury-Husson, Jules, 12
Foerster, Norman, 131
Foote, Mary Hallock, 594
Ford, Paul Leicester, 804, 846, 850; 77
Fothergill, Jessie, 454, 483, 529; 78-79
Foxton, E., 84
France, Anatole, 726
Francis, S. M., 836, 837, 839
Francois, Louise von, 273
Frederic, Harold, 824
Freeman, Mary E. Wilkins, *see* Wilkins, Mary E.
French, Harry W., 553
Freytag, Gustave, 546; 126
Fuller, Henry B., 780, 806; 36

Gaborian, M., 178
Gagneur, M. L., 568
Garland, Hamlin, 744, 812; 131
Gaskell, Mrs. Elizabeth, 761, 818
Gautier, Théophile, 102, 478, 500, 672, 843; 110, 126
Gift, Theo, 303

183

Criticism of Fiction

Gissing, George, 100
Gobineau, Le Comte de, 261
Goethe, Johann Wolfgang von, 80, 82, 323
Gogol, Nikolai, 212
Goncourt, Edmond and Jules de, 368, 465, 686
Gontcharoff, Alexander, 388
Gordon, Clarence, 226; 70
Gray, Robertson, 235; 19
Gréville, Henry, 352, 353, 387, 391, 415, 435, 443, 457
Griffiths, Arthur, 498
Gualdo, Luigi, 475
Guerrazzi, F. D., 5; 47
Gutzkow, Karl, 177

Habberton, John, 408
Hale, Edward Everett, 106, 325, 638; 14, 105
Haliburton, Thomas Chandler, 16, 752; 98
Haller, Gustave, 355, 392
Hamerton, Philip Gilbert, 336
Hamilton, Gail, see Dodge, Mary A.
Hapgood, Isabel F., 673, 733
Hardy, A r t h u r Sherburne, 593, 662, 701; 110
Hardy, Thomas, 223, 256, 310, 428, 551, 755; 19, 45-46, 55, 58, 71, 99, 125
Harrington, George F., 93
Harris, Joel Chandler, 741
Harris, Mrs. Sidney, 183
Harrison, Mrs. Burton, 775, 807
Harte, Bret, 100, 120, 161, 331, 398, 412, 577, 601, 829; 14, 46, 70, 90, 125
Haussarek, F., 451
Hawthorne, Julian, 265, 349, 591, 611, 656

Hawthorne, Nathaniel, 26, 28, 68, 105, 129, 149, 151, 152, 154, 166, 185, 197, 477, 583, 630, 656, 766, 813; 11, 31, 42-43, 63, 65
Hay, John, 609
Healy, Mary, 205
Heller, Robert, 4
Helmholtz, Hermann Ludwig von, 132
Henry, Maria Louise, 564, 581, 598
Héricault, Charles d', 192
Heusy, Paul, 460
Heyse, Paul, 436, 765
Higginson, Thomas Wentworth, 72, 74, 75, 85, 86, 115, 166, 234, 630, 847, 855; 13, 16, 67
Hillard, G. S., 9, 49, 59, 129; 12, 41, 98
Hillern, Wilhelmine von, 482
Holland J. G., 40, 297; 75, 105
Holme, Saxe, see Jackson, Helen Hunt
Holmes, Oliver Wendell, 42, 68; 14, 48, 105
Hopkinson, F. C., 34
Hosmer, Margaret, 74
House, E. H., 23, 674, 680
Houssaye, Arsene, 12
Howard, Blanche Willis, 643
Howe, E. W., 627; 57, 71
Howe, J. W., 47
Howe, M. de Wolfe, 854
Howells, William Dean, reviews of Howells' work, 563, 572, 578, 600, 641, 660, 710, 732, 756, 790, 811, 853; reviews by Howells, 89, 94, 96, 98, 103, 104, 106, 109, 111, 112, 113, 114, 116, 117, 118, 120, 132, 136, 139, 141, 144, 148, 163, 164, 165, 176, 179, 180, 184, 185, 190, 194, 203, 204, 210, 211, 220, 222, 227, 236, 244, 247, 250,

184

Index

251, 252, 260, 264, 275, 285, 295, 307, 338, 339, 343, 364, 366, 380, 381, 449, 450, 476, 477, 490, 517; comments on Howells' work, 24, 52, 59, 79-81, 89-90, 130; comments by Howells, 13-14, 15, 17, 18, 19, 20, 21-22, 33, 35-36, 42, 43, 44, 45, 46, 48, 49, 50, 55, 56, 64, 66, 67, 69, 70, 74, 87, 88, 91, 99, 105-106
Hughes, Thomas, 21, 46
Hugo, Victor, 55, 245, 288; 26, 126

Ingelow, Jean, 75, 213, 467, 639; 23, 67, 75, 127
Irving, Washington, 38, 59, 67, 479

Jackson, Helen Hunt, 411, 628; 78
James, Henry, reviews of James's works, 275, 298, 341, 381, 421, 448, 501, 549, 571, 592, 658, 694, 719, 772; reviews by James, 92, 127, 159, 265, 320, 573, 602, 632; comments on James's works, 34-35, 50, 52, 82, 100-101, 105, 118, 130, 135, 136; comments by James, 23, 27, 28, 29, 30, 32, 33, 45, 49, 56, 66, 68
Janvier, Thomas A., 748
Jay, W. L. M., 270
Jennings, L. J., 229
Jensen, Wilhelm, 363
Jewett, Sarah Orne, 339, 489, 612, 619, 730, 778; 19, 20, 22, 49, 50, 58, 88
Joanne, Adolphe, 196
Jones, Charles Henry, 308
Judd, Sylvester, 148, 505; 17, 70, 103
Juncker, E., 416

Keary, Anne, 496
Keeler, Ralph, 137, 144, 236; 75
Keenan, Henry F., 634; 57
Kent, James, 426
King, Grace, 781
Kingsley, Charles, 338
Kingsley, Henry, 57, 77, 301
Kip, Leonard, 231, 555
Kipling, Rudyard, 851
Kirk, Ellen Olney, 690, 803; 80-81
Kirk, S o p h i a, 542-545, 683, 697, 714-18, 723, 726, 727, 734-36, 739, 753, 790; 73, 80-81
Kirkland, Joseph, 699; 31
Krockow, Lida, 737, 764, 765, 785, 819; 71, 96

Laffan, Mary, 527
Lander, Meta, 86
Lanier, Sidney, 101
Lathrop, G e o r g e Parsons, 197, 219, 221, 246, 253, 258, 289, 290, 297, 298, 299, 305, 310, 312, 322, 325, 332, 333, 334, 341, 342, 346, 349, 360, 575, 583, 584-87, 599, 608-12, 614, 616, 623, 685; 19, 21, 22, 23, 25, 27, 29-30, 31, 32-33, 39, 47, 48-49, 50-51, 54-55, 56, 57, 59, 60, 64, 65-66, 71, 75-76, 77, 81, 82, 87, 88-89, 97, 99, 134-35
Lathrop, Rose Hawthorne, 813
Lavedan, Henri, 714
Le Fanu, J. S., 79, 281
Lee, Margaret, 585
Lemonnier, Camille, 274; 106
Lie, Jonas, 188
Llewellyn, E. L., 30
Lockhart, J. C., 414
Loti, Pierre, 739

185

Criticism of Fiction

Lowell, James Russell, **5, 22, 26, 37, 40, 42;** 12, 42, 43, 47, 63, 75, 98
Lowell, Robert T. S., **9, 446, 709;** 41, 114
Ludwig, Otto, 3
Luska, Sidney, 647, 678

MacClaren, Ian, 835
Macquoid, Mrs. K. S., **279**
McCarthy, Justice, 123
McClelland, M. G., **654, 670**
McGregor, Annie L., **107**
McNally, D. R., **692**
Mallock, W. H., **382, 518, 564**
Martin, C l a r a Barnes, **438, 463,** 631; 32
Marzials, Frank T., **622**
Matthews, Brander, **648, 750**
Matthiessen, F. O., 95
Mayo, W. S., **217**
Melville, Herman, 99, 134
Meredith, George, **685, 794**
Mérimée, Prosper, 598
Merwin, Henry Childs, **789**
Mitchell, D. G., 67
Mitchell, Robert E., 94, 133
Mitchell, S. Weir, **544, 625, 850;** 68-69
Mitford, Mary Russell, **169, 588,** 760
Montgomery, Florence, 199
Moore, D. A., **494**
Moore, George, 100
Morse, Clara Frances, 423
Moses, Adolf, **587**
Mott, Frank Luther, 5
Moulton, Louise Chandler, **253**
Muller, Herbert, quoted, 101
Murfree, Mary Noailles, **616, 626,** 642, 668, 700, 754; 19, 21, 34, 36, 49-50, 57, 58, 91, 121

Nadal, A. S., **237**
Noble, Annette Lucille, **513**
Nordhoff, Charles, 62, 110; 13
Norton, Charles Eliot, **31;** 11-12, 55

Oliphant, Mrs., **603, 633, 842**
O'Reilly, John Boyle, **469**
Osborn, J. D., **71**
Ouida, *see* Ramée, Marie Louise de la

Paalzow, Madame Henrietta, **480**
Page, Thomas Nelson, **740**
Pardoe, Miss, 24
Parker, Gilbert, **771, 826**
Parker, W. B., **851**
Parrington, Vernon, 135
Parsons, George Frederic, **657**
Pater, Walter, **640, 839**
Paulding, James K., **98**
Payn, James, **413, 682**
Peabody, Elizabeth P., **105**
Peard, Frances Mary, **552**
Pennot, Peter, **311**
Perkins, James Breck, **672**
Perry, Alice, **402**
Perry, Bliss, **766, 809**
Perry, Nora, **545**
Perry, Thomas Sergeant, **150, 153,** 173, 174, 177, 178, 187, 195, 196, 200, 202, 207-209, 225, 233, 238, 239, 241, 245, 248, 249, 257, 259, 261, 262, 263, 268, 273, 274, 283, 286, 288, 291, 292, 294, 296, 300, 302, 304, 313, 317, 318, 323, 326, 328, 329, 335, 337, 340, 344, 345, 347, 352, 356, 362, 363, 365, 369, 370, 388-93, 432-37, 460, 461, 462, 464, 478, 481, 482, 491, 492-503, 538, 546, 547; 17, 18-19, 21, 24, 25, 26-27, 28, 29, 30, 32, 33, 45,

Index

46, 49, 52, 56, 63-64, 68, 69, 70, 72, 73, 74, 75, 81, 82, 87, 94, 134
Peterson, Henry, 232
Phelps, Elizabeth Stuart, 121, 371, 471, 567, 604, 713, 722, 746
Picard, George H., 651
Pierce, Gilbert A., 492
Pierce, Mrs. Zina Fay, 242
Pisemski, Alexis, 150
Poe, Edgar Allan, 63
Porter, Mrs. A. E., 444
Presbury, B. F., 12
Prescott, Harriet E., *see* Spofford, Harriet Prescott
Preston, Harriet Waters, 222, 255, 266, 267, 303, 321, 336, 371-78, 382-87, 394-426, 428-31, 439-48, 451-58, 466-74, 480, 518, 633, 639, 661, 666, 675, 681, 803, 835, 838, 842, 849, 853; 18, 20, 29, 36, 39, 43, 45, 46, 48, 52, 55-56, 64-65, 80, 82, 87, 88
Prince, Helen Choate, 840
Putnam, Eleanor, 665
Putnam, G. W., 38
Pyle, Howard, 650; 28

Rabusson, Henri, 715
Ramée, Marie Louise de la, 661
Read, Emily, 636
Reade, Charles, 1, 14, 23, 50, 69, 94, 104, 165, 224, 357, 674, 680, 833; 40, 45, 47-48, 66, 114, 123, 124-25
Reclus, Elie, 368
Reeves, Marion, 636
Reid, Christian, 146, 263, 277
Repplier, Agnes, 704, 725, 731; 68, 83, 109
Reuter, Fritz, 268
Richardson, Samuel, 323; 66-67
Richter, J. P., 60, 83

Riddell, Mrs. J. H., 278
Ritchie, Anna Cora, 8
Ritchie, Mrs. Richmond, 221
Robinson, Rowland, 800
Rod, Eduoard, 718; 132
Roe, A. S., 35
Roe, E. P., 266
Round, W. M. F., 497
Rousseau, Jean Jacques, 323
Ruffini, 131; 18
Rydberg, Victor, 112

Sand, George, 47, 145, 195, 209, 318, 582; 19, 125-26
Sargent, Epes, 64
Sargent, W., 13
Savage, M. J., 407
Schreiner, Olive, 681
Schofield, William Henry, 858
Schorer, Mark, 34
Scott, Sir Walter, 6, 503, 724, 779; 33
Scudder, Horace E., 293, 358, 483-89, 504-16, 519-37, 539-41, 542, 548-62, 569, 571, 572, 574, 575, 577-80, 588, 590-97, 600, 601, 603-607, 617-21, 624-28, 634-37, 640-55, 658-60, 662-65, 667-71, 676-79, 689-93, 695, 696, 698-703, 705-11, 719-22, 724, 728-30, 732, 754, 756, 758, 770-78, 780-83, 787, 788, 799, 801, 802, 804-11, 815, 823, 830, 834, 841; 17, 19, 21, 22, 24, 25, 26, 28-29, 31, 34-35, 39-40, 49, 50, 51, 52, 53-54, 57, 58, 59, 60, 64, 67-68, 70, 71, 75, 76, 77-78, 79-80, 82-83, 87, 89-90, 91-92, 93, 97
Scudder, M. L., Jr., 422
Sedgwick, A. G., 215; 45
Sedgwick, Henry D., Jr., 814, 845, 856, 857; 35, 93

187

Criticism of Fiction

Serao, Matilde, **763, 768**
Sheppard, Elizabeth, **54, 58**
Shorey, Paul, **822;** 36, 47, 93-94, 113
Sienkiewicz, Henryk, **838**
Slick, Jonathan, *see* Haliburton, Thomas Chandler
Slosson, Annie Trumbull, **728**
Smart, Charles, **230**
Smart, Hawley, **128, 134;** 124
Smith, Bernard, 136
Smith, E. Hopkinson, **817**
Smollett, Tobias, 13
Spangler, Helen King, **294**
Sparhawk, Frances Campbell, **560**
Spielhagen, Friedrich, **140, 356, 764;** 75, 96, 117
Spofford, Harriet Prescott, **22, 54, 69, 72, 186;** 13, 115
Sprague, Mary A., **473**
Steel, Flora Annie, **837**
Steele, Mrs. C. A., **124**
Stendhal, *see* Beyle, Henri
Sterne, Laurence, **789**
Stevenson, Edward Iranaeus, **703**
Stevenson, Robert Louis, **683, 798, 848**
Stimson, Frederick J., **618**
Stockton, Frank, **509, 663, 667, 751, 805;** 24
Stoddard, Charles W., **829**
Stoddard, Elizabeth, **702**
Stoddard, W. O., **495**
Stowe, Harriet Beecher, **56, 163, 171, 181, 289, 397, 427, 821, 827;** 12, 15-16, 65
Stretton, Hesba, **385**
Sudermann, Hermann, **819;** 71-72
Sullivan, T. R., **649**
Swift, John Franklin, **133**
Symonds, W. L., **36;** 39
Synge, W. W. Follett, **379**

Tautphoeus, Baroness, **784**
Taylor, Bayard, **65, 66, 88, 189;** 13-14, 55, 74
Tenney, E. P., **406**
Thackeray, Miss, *see* Ritchie, Mrs. Richmond
Thackeray, William Makepeace, **66, 76, 117, 147, 450, 581, 684;** 31, 46, 49, 95-96
Thanet, Octave, **743, 776;** 36
Theuriet, André, **461, 488**
Thompson, C h a r l e s Miner, **800, 812, 816, 817, 832, 852;** 22, 60-61, 99
Thompson, M. L., **784**
Thoreson, Magdalen, **142**
Tiernan, Mary Spear, **653**
Tincker, M. A., **430, 558**
Tolstoy, Leo, **418, 673, 733**
Tourgée, Albion W., **487, 516, 539;** 74, 76
Towner, Ausburn, **370**
Trafton, Adelaide, **269**
Trebor, **439**
Trent, William P., **794-96, 828;** 53
Trollope, Anthony, **70, 241, 312, 359, 532, 606;** 23, 24-25, 31, 37, 109
Trollope, T. Adolphus, **99, 243;** 14, 109
Trowbridge, J. T., **37, 214, 793, 797**
Tuckerman, H. T., **99;** 14
Turgénieff, Ivan, **174, 194, 202, 207, 208, 211, 219, 220, 239, 254, 286, 291, 347, 463, 602, 631, 675;** 31, 32-33, 37, 42, 45, 56, 64-65, 71, 74, 82, 92, 115, 120, 126-27
Twain, Mark, *see* Clemens, Samuel

Uchard, Marie, **434**
Ulbach, Louis, **433**

188

Index

Underwood, F. H., **17, 260, 793**; 40-41, 67

Valerio, Katherine, **160**
Van Loon, Mrs. Elizabeth, **524**
Vance, Wilson J., **556**
Verga, C., **791**
Vincent, Leon, **843, 848**
Walford, L. B., **528**
Walford, Mrs., **639**
Wallace, Lew, **550**
Ward, Herbert D., **713, 722**
Ward, Mrs. Humphry, **695, 757, 808, 830**; 35, 77-78, 91
Warner, Charles Dudley, **364, 479, 589, 711, 712, 801, 827**; 23, 33, 51, 53, 59, 64, 70, 83
Warner, Susan and Anna, **316, 326**
Wasson, D. A., **80, 82**
Waterston, A. M., **61**
Webb, C. H., **97**
Weiss, J., **60, 83**
Wendell, Barrett, **637**
Werner, E., **365**

Wetherell, Elizabeth, **34**
Weyman, Stanley, **786**
Whipple, Edwin Percy, **28, 33, 45, 48, 50, 51, 55, 56, 76, 95, 125, 309, 319, 324, 348, 351**; 11, 12, 25, 41, 42, 71
White, Eliza Orne, **816**
Whitney, Mrs. A. D. T., **170, 504**; 51-52
Whittaker, Frederic, **400**
Wilkins, Mary E., **729, 788, 823, 852**; 22, 33-34, 36
Winchester, Carroll, **514**
Winthrop, Theodore, **44, 48, 51, 62**; 12, 13
Woodberry, George E., **687, 694**
Woods, George Bryant, **216**
Woolson, Constance Fenimore, **285, 499, 574, 595, 669, 708**; 17, 52

Zola, Emile, **340, 393, 438, 464, 491, 538**; 26-27, 28, 30, 37, 72, 74

189